THE BHAGAVAD GĪTĀ

A Verse Translation

By Brian Hodgkinson

Books For All
(an imprint of Low Price Publications)
Delhi-110052

Distributed by
D.K. Publishers Distributors (P) Ltd.
4834/24, Ansari Road, Darya Ganj,
New Delhi-110002
Phones: 23278584, 23278368, 23261465,
e-mail: dkpd@del3.vsnl.net.in
visit us at: www.dkpd.com

First Published 2003

ISBN 81-7386-262-1

Published by
Books For All
(an imprint of Low Price Publications)
A-6, Nimri Commercial Centre,
Near Ashok Vihar Phase-IV,
Delhi-110052
Phones: 27401672, 27452453
e-mail: lpp@nde.vsnl.net.in
visit us at: www.lppindia.com

Printed at
D K Fine Art Press P Ltd.
Delhi-110052

PRINTED IN INDIA

Contents

Acknowledgements

My thanks are due to Mr David Stollar and Dr Stephen Thompson for their generous assistance with several aspects of this translation. Mr Barrington Barber kindly contributed the artwork. Mr David Hodgkinson, my son, has also helped in numerous ways for which I am most grateful. My wife Catherine has been a constant support and inspiration.

Brian Hodgkinson,
Oxford, 2003

Translator's Note

The most common form of verse in the *Mahābhārata* and therefore in the *Gītā* is the *śloka*. This consists of two lines, each of sixteen syllables, which are then further divided into two halves of eight syllables with a caesura. Metre is determined by quantity: long vowels (and those before conjunct consonants) called *guru*, and short vowels called *laghu*. Thus the system is similar to that in Latin and Greek, but unlike that in English verse, which uses stress as the principal determinant of metre. In all probability epic was sung rather than spoken, and in India verses of the *Gītā* are still chanted in the traditional way.

The English verse form used in this translation makes no attempt to reproduce the metre of the Sanskrit, but rather uses iambic pentameters, following the tradition of English epic verse. The text of the *Gītā* itself contains a number of metres, but in the translation the iambic pentameter has been used throughout.

In places where there are differing interpretations of the text, Śaṃkara's commentary has been an invaluable guide.

Introduction

In the philosophical tradition of which it forms a central part the *Bhagavad Gītā* (*The Song of the Lord*) is classified as Smṛti or works derived from the memory of those who know the Veda. Smṛti forms one of the four conditions required as tests to confirm any matter of truth which may arise. Prior to Smṛti is Śruti, which refers to the Veda itself, the very source of the tradition. The Veda - the linguistic root of which is vid (to know) - is not itself a written work, but rather knowledge which is said to be coeval with mankind. Śruti (by derivation, that which is heard) is revelation based directly upon the Veda and passed down for the benefit of humanity by an oral tradition. The *Gītā* itself refers to this:

"To Vivasvat,
I gave this yoga, free from time's decay;
He taught it then to Manu, who in turn
Taught King Ikṣvāku, first Kṣatriya.
To every mighty ruler it descends,
Until within the long expanse of time
It seems to perish."

(IV,1,2)

The Upanishads are the quintessence of the Śruti. The third condition is the teaching of a self-realized man, such as those in a direct line of discipleship from the original

Śaṃkarācārya, who wrote commentaries on the scriptures and taught the system of Advaita philosophy. The final test of truthfulness is the experience of the man himself who is confronted with the question or problem at issue. Without this he would be unable to recognize fully the validity of the answer; it would not be accepted, as it were, in the heart. The agreement of Śruti, Smṛti, the self-realized man and the individual, therefore, guarantees the truthfulness of an answer to any question. It is the seal of truth[1].

Memory as the source of what is written in the Smṛti is not merely the recalling of what has been learnt in the past. Rather it is bringing to mind what is known inherently within oneself as an aspect of one's own being. It is a kind of re-membering or unifying of what has been dismembered or scattered by the distractions of life in the world. Plato expressed this as the recollection of pre-natal knowledge. Whatever is known before birth and after death is known eternally. If time is understood only as a condition of embodied life, then such knowledge is not subject to time and is indeed available to be discovered in the present. Authors of Smṛti are those who have made the discovery.

The *Gītā* is in fact an extract from the vast epic of *The Mahābhārata*, a work of 88,000 verses in its shortest recension and the longest epic in any language. The author was the sage, Vyāsa, who was said to have given celestial sight to Sañjaya, the narrator of much of the story, including the *Gītā* itself, in order that he could describe the events to the blind king, Dhṛtarāṣṭra. Essentially the *Gītā* is a philosophical dialogue between Kṛṣṇa and Arjuna, taking place on the battlefield of Kurukṣetra, just before the battle begins between the Pāṇḍavas and the Kauravas. A long-standing feud has brought these two branches of a common

---

1. *Laws of Manu* II, 6, 10

family to this final bloody resolution. Duryodhana, eldest son of Dhṛtarāṣṭra, becomes uncontrollably jealous of the five sons of his uncle, Paṇḍu, and attempts to kill them in a fire from which they escape. Dhṛtarāṣṭra, however, seeks reconciliation and bestows land upon the Pāṇḍava brothers, who build themselves a great palace at Indraprastha, where the eldest, Yudhiṣṭhira, is crowned. Once more Duryodhana's jealousy is inflamed, and this time an evil counsellor advises him to challenge the Pāṇḍavas to a game of dice. For all his great virtues, Yudhiṣṭhira has a weakness for gambling. He loses all his wealth, and stakes his brothers and himself, but loses yet again. In desperation he even stakes Princess Draupadī, who is the wife of all five brothers. Of course, he loses; moreover, Draupadī is grossly insulted by a courtier who tries to disrobe her. Only a miraculous never-ending robe saves her from humiliation. Nevertheless, the five brothers and their wife lose their kingdom and are banished to the forest for twelve years, followed by a year of wandering as unknown strangers.

When the Pāṇḍavas eventually return, they seek to reclaim their rightful kingdom by negotiation, but Duryodhana will not grant them even a sliver of land. They prepare for war. At this point the Lord Kṛṣṇa, a nephew of Paṇḍu, intervenes, but even his peace-loving eloquence cannot persuade the implacable Duryodhana to be reconciled with his cousins. Thus the armies assemble upon the plains of Kurukṣetra, the field of the Kuru dynasty, to which the respective leaders belong. It is here that Arjuna, the third son and the greatest archer of his time, experiences the terrible grief which gives rise to the dialogue of the *Gītā*. Kṛṣṇa is his charioteer. Yet, as his attempts to keep the peace suggest, Kṛṣṇa is more than another participant in the feud. Indeed, he is an incarnation of God, come into the world at a time of great trouble to bring ease to those who suffer[2]. When Arjuna turns to him, he responds in full and teaches him the whole life-giving philosophy of the Vedic tradition.

For eighteen days the battle rages across the plain, marked, as always in war, by the degeneration of the high standards of heroic conduct, until at the end both sides resort to lies and unnecessary cruelty. Even Yudhiṣṭhira, the epitomy of the noble Kṣhatriya[3], stoops to tell a falsehood in order to weaken the resolve of the Kaurava commander. Finally, after a series of duels and massacres, only the five Pāṇḍava brothers, Kṛṣṇa and one other survive. Yudhiṣṭhira rules over the devastated kingdom under the nominal king, Dhṛtarāṣṭra, and the sage, Vyāsa, manages to reconcile at last the Pāṇḍavas and the Kauravas. Many years later Kṛṣṇa by his own choice leaves the world, and soon after the Pāṇḍava brothers die. The last of them, Yudhiṣṭhira, finds that his brothers and Draupadī are not in heaven and chooses to leave, imagining that they are in hell, but later all are reunited in heaven, where too they are finally reconciled with the Kauravas.

According to the tradition to which the *Mahābhārata* itself belongs, this epic feud and battle took place at the end of the Bronze Age, the third epoch of the four which form a mahāyuga or great cycle of time. In the Golden Age men are simple and peaceful, living in harmony with themselves and others, free of egoism and any form of vice. In the Silver Age which follows, the idea of "me" and "mine" has reared its head, but a sense of moral duty is strongly held, and the leadership of kings, advised by wise men, holds the community fast to the law and to ancient custom. The succeeding Bronze Age is marked by the presence of heroic warriors, intent upon honour and glory,

2. *Gītā* IV, 7-8

3. See Note on *Castes*.

magnanimous and energetic, but prone to such vices as ambition, cruelty and revenge. Inevitably theirs is a society of feud and warfare, though capable of high culture and, of course, heroic deeds. Kurukṣetra denotes the end of the Bronze Age[4]. The very degeneration of the battle demonstrates the declining virtue of the protagonists, their relapse into selfish motives as they forget the moral code of their ancestors. Indeed, Arjuna's grief is more than the cry of a man who may lose his family and friends and must himself take part in the killing. It is the profound despair of one who feels himself to be an agent in the downfall of mankind itself, a cause of the secular deterioration of human life:

> "Can we, who know this law, ignore the crime?
> When families fall their ancient rites are lost
> And, losing sight of law, they are destroyed
> By lack of righteousness."
>
> (I, 39-40)

It is little wonder that it takes Kṛṣṇa so long to lead Arjuna to the point where his doubt is resolved and he can fight with confidence. The issue is not one of cowardice, nor of sympathy, nor even of love for his fellows; it is the perennial problem of all who find themselves taking part in destructive actions that appear to jeopardize the future of humanity, from Kurukṣetra to Hiroshima.

What follows the Age of Bronze is that of Iron. This final age of mankind witnesses the full degradation which humanity can experience. It takes time before the full catalogue of terrible abuses is enacted - the gratuitous

---

4. In the tradition of western literature, the siege of Troy in Homer's *Iliad* may be seen as occupying the same place as that of the battle of Kurukshetra in Sanskrit literature. The Bronze Age - which Hesiod and Ovid, for example, describe - is ending, and the greatest heroes of the time from all over the Greek world confront each other in destructive war before the walls of Troy. See Note on *Yuga*.

violence, the exploitation of the weak, the sexual precocity of children, the corruption of all in authority, and so on - but initially there is a period (called sandhi) when these are foreshadowed. The saving grace of the Iron Age is that the memory of the truth is not totally obliterated[5]. Indeed, for some men the very horror of the Iron Age is an opportune reminder to seek the truth. Moreover, God has provided for the needs of mankind, even in the darkness of the time, by the presence of an incarnation who teaches the holy tradition of the Veda. In the West there is Christ; in the East there is Kṛṣṇa. Hence the *Song of the Lord* is sung at the most auspicious moment, when, as the Bronze Age gives way to Iron, the final resort of all men is a teaching which will sustain them in the wilderness that the collapse of civilization has engendered.

What then is the holy tradition, or sacred law? It is the vehicle for the philosophy of Advaita, or non-dualism[6], the central doctrine of which is the Oneness of all. No other, not other people, not the created world in its entirety, nor even God, is separate from oneself:

> "For on Myself this universe is strung,
> Like jewels, O son of Kunti, on a thread."
>
> (VII, 7)

The conscious Self contains the whole of creation: what is manifested to the senses as matter, what is contained in the mind, and what is unmanifest, which is the potentiality of things or what Plato understood as Ideas or Forms. Consciousness is indivisible like space; any part of it is not really separate from any other part, any more than the space in a pot is really separate from the rest of space. Moreover, this consciousness is the reality in everything

---

5. See *Śrīmad Bhāgavatam* (King Parīkṣhit meets Kali)

6. For the six philosophical systems which have been used to interpret the *Gītā*, see A.L Basham, *The Wonder that.was India*, pp. 323-328.

that it pervades. The rest is no more than illusion or Māyā[7], which is a kind of dream within the one consciousness. Everything that appears to exist, objects and their qualities, are ultimately no more than names and forms, and even these have no real existence. For the mark of reality is to be changeless. All forms change; they seem to come into and go out of existence, but, according to the *Gītā*, nothing can really do so. Whatever exists has always existed and will always exist; whatever does not exist never has existed and never will. Hence the only reality is the Self, which is one and the same as consciousness. The *Gītā* echoes the *Kaṭha Upaniṣad*[8] when it asserts the eternity of the Self:

> "Self is not born, nor does it ever die;
> It does not come to life, not having been,
> Nor, having been, does it thereafter cease."
>
> (II, 20)

The Self and Māyā might be thought of as distinct and therefore the constituents of dualism. This would be to misunderstand the nature of Māyā. It has no reality; it is totally dependent for its apparent existence upon the real, which is consciousness. Remove consciousness, remove the Self, and there is nothing. Māyā is like a picture on a cinema screen, beguiling, realistic, easy to identify with, but ephemeral and completely wiped out the instant the light is turned off. To claim that I or someone else really lives in the world is as huge an error as to claim that I can physically get into a car on the screen and drive out of the cinema!

The idea of the unity of the Self presents a problem to the twentieth century mind, which is firmly convinced that it exists as the mind of an individual self. Yet everything

---

7. See Note on *Māyā*.

8. *Katha Upanishad* I, 2, 18. Cf. also the pre-Socratic, Melissus (J. Barnes, *Early Greek Philosophy*, p. 145)

that differentiates people one from another - their bodies, their thoughts, their feelings, however subtle they may be - can be observed. The observation itself has nothing which differentiates it. Even observation apparently from a particular place and time, which seems so compelling a reason for believing that one is in fact a separate being, depends upon the differentiation of observed things such as viewpoints or measurements of time. The pure observation itself cannot be differentiated. Hence it is one, the same in all observers. The *Gītā* says this with poetic licence:

> " . . . . but It envelops all,
> Possessed of hands and feet in every place,
> And eyes and heads and mouths, with ears that hear
> Throughout the universe, and yet, in truth,
> Possessing none, but shining through them all.
> Quite unattached and yet supporting all,
> Devoid of qualities, outside all things -
> The moving and unmoved - and yet within,
> Too fine to be perceived, far off yet near,
> As though divided into many parts,
> It yet remains its undivided Self,"
>
> (XIII, 13-16)

Yet such a thoroughgoing unity seems to fly completely in the face of experience. Is each person not a separate conscious entity, aware of the world about him and of other people as similarly conscious entities with whom each communicates through a commonly agreed language and by other means? That is indeed the common-sense view, though it may not have been in other cultures than ours. Does that view, however, stand up to even a little examination? Are my body and my inner states, like feelings and thoughts, part of the conscious entity which I call myself or are they a part of the otherness of which I am aware? Clearly, in so far as I am aware of them, they are not myself. Marsilio Ficino, the leading philosopher of the Florentine Renaissance, expressed this point in a letter to his friend, Cavalcanti:

> "I have often looked for myself, Giovanni. First I have touched my chest with my hands, then I have often gazed at this face in the mirror, but I could never say that I have touched myself with the one or seen myself in the other. For, when I seek myself, I am certainly not looking for another but for him who seeks. Indeed, it is exactly the same Marsilio that is both seeker and sought. Who does the seeking? He who wishes to discover. Who wants to discover? He who knows that there is something worth looking for. Who knows this? Why, spirit alone. So it is spirit alone I seek, since I seek myself, who am indeed pure spirit. This I well know can be neither touched nor seen. For we would not be in doubt about its nature for so long, if it were accessible to these senses. Then, too, whenever I have drawn the sharp sight of the mind back to itself, hoping that I might see myself in this way, I have by no means thus attained what I desired."
>
> (*The Letters of Marsilio Ficino*, Vol. I, p. 78; trans. School of Economic Science)

Ficino's conclusion that the self is a spirit was not shared, however, by the Scottish philosopher, David Hume, who used a similar argument about the imperceptibility of the self. Hume's conclusion was that the concept of the self is no more than a product of the imagination, which is compelled to postulate such an entity as a result of the incessant habitual impressions which are associated together as mine. In which case there is no more a real self than there is a real cause of anything, for causes also are, on

Hume's view, no more than the imagination's way of dealing with constant conjunctions of phenomena[9]. Hume's scepticism has been enormously influential, of course, in attenuating the philosophical views present in the Florentine Renaissance.

In the twentieth century Ludwig Wittgenstein drew a stronger conclusion from Hume's opinion that there is no real knowledge of an individual self. For a time Wittgenstein advocated a no-ownership theory of the self to the effect that impressions, sensations, etc. belong to no-one. From the point of view of the *Gītā* - and of Ficino - such a strange theory is not so much false as incomplete, for no-ownership leaves the objects of awareness, like sense impressions, in a kind of limbo, as entities in an impersonal world of discrete things. The teaching of Advaita does not thus eliminate individual awareness, but rather subsumes it within a greater awareness which is universal. At the same time it does not leave the objects of awareness as disconnected and ownerless things. For they too are brought within the whole nexus of conscious unity.

How is this done? The *Īśā Upaniṣad* makes a simple but profound statement:

> "The Self is one. Unmoving, it moves faster than the mind. The senses lag, but Self runs ahead. Unmoving, it outruns pursuit. Out of Self comes the breath that is the life of all things."
>
> (*The Ten Principal Upanishads*, trans. Shrī Purohit Swāmi and W.B.Yeats, p. 15)

The Self then is not the mind, for it moves faster than the mind. Yet it does not move, though it outruns pursuit. Only one answer is possible to such a riddle. Only consciousness itself can both remain where it is and outpace

---

9. D. Hume, *A Treatise on Human Nature*, III, SII-I; IV, SVI

the mind and the senses; and it can only do this if it is everywhere at once, so that it does not move and yet "gets to" any place before anything else at all which has to travel there. This Self then is consciousness. It cannot be an atom-like point within each individual, for that could hardly travel anywhere, except perhaps mounted in the ponderous vehicle of the body. In which case the Self must be a universal consciousness, present at all places, and by implication at all times also:

> "What is this homogenous Brahman? This self. What is that? The inner self that sees, hears, thinks, understands, knows; the perceiver of everything, because as the self of all it perceives everything. This is the teaching of all Vedānta texts - the gist of them. It leads to immortality and fearlessness."
>
> (*Bṛhadāraṇyaka Upaniṣad II,19; Commentary by Śaṃkarācārya*, trans. Svāmi Madhavānda)

What evidence is there for this? In the ordinary sense of evidence, there cannot possibly be any. Anything that could be pointed to as evidence would itself be an object of consciousness and therefore not appropriate. The lack of evidence for an individual self as the subject of experience is, of course, a pointer, but there is a better case to be made than this. If a universal consciousness is taken to be the Self - the one Self in the hearts of all - then the philosophical difficulties associated with dualism are found to be dissolved. There are, for example, no problems arising from the existence of more than one substance, in the philosophical sense of an irreducible entity totally independent of other such entities and in which qualities inhere. The Cartesian problem of the relationship between the two substances of mind and body does not then exist. Since both minds and bodies are within the one consciousness their relationship takes place within, as it were, a common medium. Similarly the problem of how people can communicate with each other if each is an atomistic self-dependent entity, ultimately separate from every other - as presented in such modern authors as Kafka and Sartre, for example - is avoided by the simple solution of non-separation in a common consciousness which underlies all human relationships.

Wittgenstein has again provided a kind of partial case for the unity of consciousness in his argument against the possibility of a private language[10]. Suppose there were such a language, he postulates. Then, whenever a certain sort of event occurred in my experience, I might write down a sign which represented this event for me, but which no-one else could connect with such a type of event, because the meaning of the sign was in principle known only to me. When the event recurred, I should write down the same sign. What however does the word "same" do in this context? Only I can be the judge of sameness. In which case there cannot be a distinction between my using the sign correctly and using it incorrectly. I cannot make a mistake, and therefore I cannot be correct either, for the idea of correctness depends upon the possibility of my being incorrect, at least sometimes. In other words there is no rule for the use of the sign; thus it is not a word in a language. It has no meaning.

If a private language is impossible, is not private experience impossible also by the same kind of argument? For what are the experiences themselves that are said to be logically private? How are they identified and re-identified? Nothing can possibly be said of such an experience; therefore it makes little sense to claim that it exists. Of course, an empirically private experience, which as a matter of fact is concealed from others, is certainly possible. Otherwise such things as pretending, lying, deceiving and so on would be impossible.

---

10. Wittgenstein, *Philosophical Investigations*, I, 256-272

Wittgenstein was not inclined to draw the conclusion that if experience cannot ultimately be private, then it must all be "public", in the sense of inter-personal. Such a conclusion points to the philosophy of Advaita. If there is no such thing as experience which is logically or in principle private, then there is no such thing as private consciousness. Consciousness cannot be "mine" as opposed to "yours" or "his". If, on the other hand, consciousness is inter-personal, then, like space, it has a unity which transcends the apparent - and false - division into bits of private consciousness.

This argument derived from a twentieth century philosopher leads, anachronistically, to the central principle of Immanuel Kant's *Critique of Pure Reason*. Kant was not satisfied with Hume's reliance upon the imagination. He saw in the world and in himself a necessity which went beyond the powers of imagination and was recognized indeed by reason. There is, wrote Kant, an empirical unity in our experience. It seems to consist of appearances which hang together in an ordered way, such as the continuous existence of objects, like pots, and the regular occurrence of effects following causes, like a pot breaking when dropped on the ground. This unity, however, is contingent. Thought can easily eliminate it by imagining disorder, like the spontaneous disintegration of a particular object or the non-occurrence of a particular effect. Kant, however, was not satisfied with contingent unity. He was aware that experience in general requires an order. The very concept of an object or of a cause demands a necessary order. Without the necessary continuity of appearances according to a rule there would be no such concepts as object and cause. If all such things as pots might simply appear or disappear without any temporal continuity; if they might break and not break, even though the conditions were the same in each case, then the very concepts of object and cause would lose their meaning. Hence there would be nothing that could be called experience.

Yet even that is not sufficient. For experience to be intelligible it must be conscious experience; there must be an observer or witness of the experience for it to take place at all. But whose consciousness is it? Someone must be able to call it "mine". Without this "mine", it would not be intelligible as experience - it would not be experienced. Experience is then necessarily "mine"; and it can only be so if there is a necessary rule which makes it so. The rule is what Kant calls the transcendental unity of apperception. By such apperception he means the recognition of oneself as consciousness, not the merely empirical introspection which is the awareness of inner states, like thoughts and feelings. Introspection has the empirical unity of certain states being linked to others, but transcendental apperception has a necessary unity, since no experience would be possible if it could not necessarily be called "mine":

> ":................there must be a condition which precedes all experience and which makes experience itself possible. There can be in us no modes of knowledge, no connection or unity of one mode of knowledge with another, without that unity of consciousness which precedes all data of intuitions, and by relation to which representations of objects is alone possible. This pure original unchangeable consciousness I shall name transcendental apperception."
>
> (*Critique of Pure Reason*, trans. N. Kemp Smith, p. 136)

It is no great step to take Kant's concept of transcendental unity of apperception to mean the Ātman or Self of the Vedic teaching. For that Self, too, is presented by the Veda as the fundamental condition of all experience. According to the Māṇḍūkya Upaniṣad, whichever of the three states of waking, dreaming or deep sleep prevails at any time, there is also present an underlying condition - the presence of the Ātman. Hence the Self is the ever-present unity of consciousness:

> "(The Self) is the essence of the one self-cognition common to all states of consciousness."
>
> (*Māṇḍūkya Upaniṣad*, VII,
> trans. Swāmi Sarvānanda)

The doctrine of Advaita is of fine subtlety. For this reason the follower of Advaita easily falls into error, and to one particular error is he most prone. In his great commentary to the *Gītā*, the first Śaṃkarāchārya gave this warning:

> "There is, again, another sort of learning ....which may be stated as follows: the Lord Himself is the knower of the field, and the field is quite distinct from the knower who perceives it; but I am a *saṃsārin*[11] subject to pleasure and pain. To bring about the cessation of *saṃsāra*[12] I should first acquire a discriminative knowledge of the field and the knower of the field, then attain a direct perception of the knower of the field, the Lord, by means of meditation on the Lord, and then dwell in the true nature of the Lord."
>
> (Commentary to *Gītā*, XIII, 2
> trans. Alladi Mahadeva Sastry)

Whoever holds this view is "ignorant in himself, confounds others, devoid of the traditional key to the

11. Someone attached to mundane existence.
12. The circle of mundane existence; worldly life; or more strictly transmigration, which is the cyclical repetition of worldly life.

teaching." The error is to assume that one is a separate conscious existence seeking to find the Self or the Lord, when in truth one is that one Self already. The proper search is simply to find out how to rid oneself of the obstacles that cover the reality:

> "They have put a golden stopper into the neck of the bottle. Pull it, Lord! Let out reality. I am full of longing."
>
> (*Īśā Upanișhad. The Ten Principal Upanișhads*, trans. Shri Purohit Swāmi and W.B. Yeats, pp. 16-17)

As the conversation of the *Gītā* unfolds, it becomes increasingly clear to Arjuna that the only reasonable course for him, and for all men, is to discover the union with the Lord who is the Self of all. In fact, Kṛṣṇa points out more than one way by which this may be achieved. Three ways in particular are elaborated: karma yoga, bhakti yoga and jñāna yoga, corresponding, more or less, to the paths to be followed through action, devotion and intellect, but available as one way with three aspects for those who are not especially inclined to any one[13]. Kṛṣṇa indicates that jñāna yoga is the highest of these and that the others are preparations for it, though his emphasis upon how dear to him are the followers of bhakti yoga suggests that devotion alone may be sufficient[14]. In addition, there is meditation (dhyāna yoga), which by strengthening the aspirant's attention and leading ever deeper within himself complements all three ways[15].

---

13. There is a tradition that the *Gītā* may be divided into three sections, dealing respectively with karma yoga (Chs. 1-6), bhakti yoga (Chs. 7-12) and jñāna yoga (Chs. 13-18).

14. See *Gītā* XII

15. See *Gītā* VI

Karma yoga, the way of action, is referred to at the beginning of the *Īśā Upaniṣad*:

> "By doing karma, indeed, should one wish to live here for a hundred years. For a man, such as you, there is no way other than this, whereby karma may not cling to you."
>
> (I,2, trans. Swāmi Gambhirānanda)

The Śaṃkarāchārya comments that "the antithesis between knowledge and karma is irremovable like a mountain"[16]. In the *Gītā* the Lord Kṛṣṇa makes it clear to Arjuna that he is not ready to follow the way of jñāna yoga and must accept that of karma yoga. Kṛṣṇa holds out the promise, however, that a sincere follower of the latter may eventually reach a purified state suitable for jñāna yoga. Meanwhile, karma yoga has three aspects, all of which may be practised, but which themselves form a kind of hierarchy of development on the way. The lowest form is to surrender the fruits of action, that is to give up the thought that an action is to be judged or valued by its results or rewards:

> "You have the right to work, to that alone,
> To any fruits you have no claim at all."
>
> (II, 47)

In a sense the follower of karma is to act purposelessly, which does not mean aimlessly, for all actions have an aim, but rather without diverting the attention at all from the moment of action to anything consequent upon it. The expert tennis player aims to clip the white line, but his attention is totally on the ball, not on the thought of where it will land, or the applause of the crowd! Moreover, for the lover of tennis the moment of contact with the ball is valued for its own sake.

16. Commentary on *Īsā Upaniṣad*, I, 21; op. cit.

Secondly, the way of action enjoins the disciple to avoid identification with the action:

> "Steadfast in action, he thinks 'I do not act'
> In seeing, hearing, touching, smell or taste,
> In moving, sleeping, breathing in or out,
> Or in conversing, taking and in giving,
> Or even in the closing of the eyes,
> He is aware that senses merely move
> Amongst their objects."
>
> (V, 8-9)

This sounds remarkably like a statement of jñāna yoga, and, of course, it is a preparation for it, but the difference lies in the place of action in the disciple's practice. For the follower of karma yoga, action is central to his life; he is a man of action, living in the world, not a monk or recluse. Action is not to be renounced, except in the subtle respect of not identifying with it. The follower of jñāna yoga remembers "I am not the doer"; the follower of karma yoga remembers "I am not the action being done", for, as a man of action, that is his habitual mistake; he thinks he is the shooting of the arrow or the hitting of the ball, whereas in truth the shooting and the hitting, the speaking or the writing, take place according to the natural laws that govern the elements. The hand releases, or the tongue vibrates, most efficiently when there is no identification with the ego, when the action just takes place of itself. What remains is the uninvolved witness, the consciousness in the action, which is not the ego and does not interfere like the ego.

The finest form of karma yoga, however, is to offer every action to the Self or the Lord. This dedication of action is made by the mind in acknowledgement of the ultimate source of all action, from which arise all the constituents of action, the body, agent, organs, their functions and a presiding deity[17]. Dedication removes the ego from the action, since it is the ego which tries to usurp the place of the Lord Himself. A familiar trick, for example, is for the ego to pretend to be a conscious witness itself, a form, perhaps, of the cardinal sin of pride! Thus dedication is a kind of remembering of the true hierarchy, which begins in the Brahman[18] and ends in the full manifestation of the element earth, the created world of physical objects. Kṛṣṇa frequently advises Arjuna, as a man of action, to remember this highest type of karma yoga:

> "Whatever you may do, whatever eat,
> Whatever you may sacrifice, or give,
> Whatever strict austerity you choose,
> O son of Kunti, offer that to Me.
> By this the bonds of action shall be loosed,
> And thus absolved from good or bad results,
> Renouncing all, and free, come then to Me."
>
> (IX, 27-8)

The culmination of karma yoga is to penetrate deeply into the nature of action itself and to see that at its root is the presence of the Lord. For him who has achieved this penetration, action is in truth inaction and inaction action[19]. Action pivots, as it were, upon an unmoving hub, "the still point of the turning world", as T.S.Eliot put it[20], whilst inaction or inertness contains a whole range of activity of body, mind and emotion. To realize this still centre of action whilst acting is to make the action sacrificial, and by sacrificial action the path of jñāna yoga is opened:

---

17. See *Gītā* XVIII, 13-14
18. See Note on *Brahman*
19. *Gītā* IV, 18
20. *Burnt Norton*, II

"This cow of plenty quenches every thirst;
The gods, so nourished, nourish you in turn
And you shall then attain the highest good."

(III, 10-11)

Bhakti yoga is described explicitly in Chapter XII of the *Gītā*, but its spirit is often captured elsewhere in the *Gītā*, for devotion is never absent from any other way of discovering Brahman or the Lord. Without devotion how would the aspirant keep to the path of reason or of action? Yet for some people of an emotional nature, the way of devotion is especially suitable. The artist, whose aim is to melt the heart of the beholder of his work, the servant whose paramount duty is to meet every need of his master, the wife whose love for her husband overrides all else, such men and women find in the way of devotion their truest service; but the work of art, the master and the husband are not the real object of their love. What they truly love is what alone is real within the beloved:

"Of a certainty the wife does not love her husband for himself but loves him for herself only...............................

For as long as there is duality, one sees the other, one smells the other, one hears the other, one speaks to the other, one thinks of the other, one knows the other; but when everything is one Self, who can see another, how can he see another ....

How can the knower be known?"

(*Bṛhadāraṇyaka Upaniṣhad, IV. The Ten Principal Upaniṣhads*, trans. Shri Purohit Swāmi and W.B. Yeats, pp. 130-133)

To devote oneself to the impersonal Absolute, the Brahman, is difficult, for most men impossible; therefore the follower of bhakti yoga should be devoted to the Lord who dwells within all creatures, who becomes "ere long their saviour from the ocean of despair[21]." Such love for the embodied Brahman is the source of most religions. For this reason it is easy enough for religion to become thoroughly dualistic, since the apparent dualism of oneself on one side and God on the other is only too obvious. Devotion to God, if God is understood as outside or beyond oneself, has its advantages, of course, and may be a great deal better than a lack of devotion or disbelief in God, but the inner truth of religions is Advaita, as the greatest spiritual traditions make evident. As Jesus said, "I and my Father are one[22]". Love between God and the devotee is an incomplete condition, which Socrates explains in Plato's *Symposium*, for love implies a longing for something not possessed[23]. On the realization of union, or Oneness, there is no place for an in-between. Only for the ignorant can love be advocated, but all forms of yoga are for the ignorant and only for the ignorant are the *Gītā* and other scriptures written. Meanwhile, the disciple on the way of bhakti yoga takes solace from the Lord's kind words that he, the devotee, "is held most dear, highest in My esteem[24]."

Jñāna yoga, the way of knowledge, appeals to reason. When Kṛṣṇa has first upbraided Arjuna for his unmanly grief, he immediately begins to expound the teaching which reason recognizes as the resolution of the problem of suffering. He describes the reality that lies behind Arjuna's perception of pain and disaster. Pain and pleasure are transient and illusory. When the body falls the man himself

21. *Gītā*, XII, v 7

22. John, X, 30. The Gospel of John contains several other statements by Jesus with this import. The *Hymns of Śaṃkara* and the early Sufi teachings of Abu Yazid and Al-Hallaj are examples from the Hindu and Muslim traditions respectively.

23. *Symposium*, 200-203

24. *Gītā*, XII, 19

does not die, for his true Self is beyond birth and death and undergoes no change:

"………Not edge of sword,

Nor fire, nor fury of the wind, nor rain,

Touch that pure substance which pervades them all."

(II, 23-4)

Later, Kṛṣṇa analyses further the nature of that Self. Its lower nature consists of the elements which form the world: earth, water, fire, air and space; mind, reason or intellect, and ego or the sense of existence. These are universal, not individual, properties of the world; of them are constituted the particular types of element that we experience, such as the multifarious forms of earth, which we call physical substances. The higher nature of the Self is the Spirit that lies in the essence of everything, sustaining it with life and brilliance:

"I am, of limpid water, the sweet taste;

I am the radiance of Moon and Sun,

OM in all Vedas, the essential sound

Of space, and the humanity in men;

Pure scent in earth, and brilliant light of fire,

The life of every being and the zeal

Of those who undertake austerity."

(VII, 8-9)

The work of reason in jñāna yoga is to remove identification with the separate elements. Having heard the scriptural statement about the Self, or Brahman, reason becomes capable of discriminating between this - its own Self - and each element. Hence if there is identification with the physical body, as when one says, "I am hurt", reason realizes that this is not so, that it is only the element earth that is hurt and not the Self. The traditional injunction "neti, neti" ("not this, not this") is used to make this discrimination. Or if there is identification with the mind - a fairly common occurrence! - reason similarly realizes that it is only the mind, not the Self, which is full of anger, deep in thought, well-intentioned, or whatever. Historically the error of identification with the mind stems in part from the powerful influence of Descartes' argument, "cogito ergo sum" ("I think, therefore I am"). For by making thought the ground, or necessary condition, for concluding that one exists, Descartes made it only too easy for the modern mind to identify existence with thought, rather than to regard thought as itself requiring a prior ground of existence. Whereas in Sanskrit the word "Aham", meaning "I am", stands for the entry of the Absolute, or Brahman, into spatio-temporal form. Yet however strong and habitual identification with the mind may be, it can always be removed by the power of reason, for that power, the *Gītā* assures us, is a mighty fire or a sharp sword, not the cool instrument familiar to us.

Having discriminated in this way, the follower of jñāna yoga might appear to have strayed into a form of dualism far from the doctrine of Advaita; but such discrimination is, of course, only one step. It is the removal of identification with an individual element. The second step is to realize the illusory nature of what is observed as the object of consciousness, namely the element itself. Since all such elements - the lower nature of the Lord - collectively constitute Māyā, the follower of Advaita holds to the reality of the Self alone, for in that lies the Oneness which he seeks. In the famous analogy of the rope and the snake, teachers of Advaita elucidate this point. The ignorant man thinks that the rope is a snake, but when the scales fall from his eyes he sees the rope for what it is. There are not, and never were, two things - a rope and a snake. Nor does the appearance itself undergo a change. It is only the removal of ignorance which reveals the pre-existing and unchanging reality.

Since the *Gītā* gives emphasis to the doctrine of karma yoga as appropriate for such men of action as Arjuna, it is inevitable that the concept of duty should figure prominently. Kṛṣṇa enjoins Arjuna to act without thought for the results, to act for the sake of duty only, for duties are not to be renounced:

> "Freedom from action never shall be found
> By mere inaction ....
> Whatever is your duty, follow that,"
>
> (III, 4,8)

Such dutiful action is done for the good of all:

> "..................so then should you act,
> Looking to the welfare of the world."
>
> (III, 20)

In both these respects - action for duty's sake and action for the good of all - the *Gītā* is presenting a truth about moral behaviour, which Western philosophers, notably Kant, have discussed extensively. Kant's austere concept of the moral law, interpreted as a categorical imperative free from conditions, such as the desire for results or the benevolence of the moral agent, conforms to the *Gītā's* injunction (See II,47, quoted above). Moral principles, writes Kant, "expect nothing from the inclinations of man, but everything from the supremacy of the law and from the reverence due to it"[25]. The supreme principle of moral action is to "act only on that maxim through which you can at the same time will that it should become a universal law"[26]. In addition Kant deduces from his imperative

---

25. *Groundwork of the Metaphysic of Morals* (trans. H.J. Paton), p. 93
26. *ibid*, p. 88

another formulation of it which follows closely the *Gītā's* references to the "welfare of the world" and "the care of all mankind":

> "Act in such a way that you always treat humanity, whether in your own person or in the person of any other, never simply as a means, but always at the same time as an end."
>
> (*Kant, The Moral Law*, trans. H.J. Paton, p. 96)

Each man, as a rational agent, can only will a maxim as universal law if he regards all other men as ends in themselves, capable, like him, of willing universally. Thus all men are to be treated as ends in themselves; hence the man of reason acts for the care of all mankind in the performance of duty. To act for duty's sake and for the good of all are not two things but one, as the *Gītā* confirms:

> "Whilst fools forever act for selfish ends,
> Wise men, though also acting, stay unbound,
> Intent upon the care of all mankind."
>
> (III, 25)

This concept of duty clearly runs up against the deep conviction of Arjuna that he should not fight against his kinsmen and friends. Kṛṣṇa's advice, however, dwells upon the need to avoid completely all sentiment, partiality and fear. The duty of a warrior is to fight in a righteous cause. What the consequences will be are a matter for God and nature; he is not responsible for the consequences, only for his duty. He cannot know whether those he kills will go to heaven or hell. In truth, only bodies are killed, in any case; neither the Spirit in them, nor the Spirit in himself, kill or are killed. On one level, indeed, the *Gītā* is a treatise on the moral law. On another and higher level it shows that the moral law is only a necessary device for those who believe that there are many agents whom rationality brings into harmony. In this way again karma yoga is a step towards jñāna yoga, which teaches that in reality all men are one and the same. For the self-realized man there is no moral law, nor duty:

"........................but when, as rivers flow
And fill the tranquil ocean from all sides,
Desires flow into him, that man finds peace,
Longing for nothing, giving up desire,
Without a sense of "I" or what is "mine."
(II, 70-1)

Those saintly men who have discovered the Self act, like Kṛṣṇa himself, in order to show others how to act righteously, not from any motive they could call their own[27].

Chapter XII of the *Gītā* contains a description of a saṃnyāsin[28], which presents a man free from all desire and hence able to act with indifference for the good of all:

"He who is the same to friend and foe,
In honour and dishonour, heat and cold,
Unmoved in pleasure and in misery,
Free from attachment to the world of sense,
Equal in the face of praise and blame,
Imbued with silence, ever satisfied,
With no home but Myself: one such as this,
Steadfast and full of love, is dear to Me."
(XII, 18-19)

No better description could be given of a Roman follower of Stoicism, such as Seneca the Younger or Marcus Aurelius. Since Shakespeare was much influenced by Stoic ideas, particularly from Seneca, it is no surprise to find a remarkable parallel to this *Gītā* passage in Hamlet, where the prince praises his friend, Horatio:

---

27. *Gītā* III, 21-24

28. See Note on *Saṃnyāsin*

"......................for thou hast been
As one, in suff'ring all, that suffers nothing,
A man that Fortune's buffets and rewards
Hast ta'en with equal thanks; and blest are those
Whose blood and judgment are so well comeddled
That they are not a pipe for Fortune's finger
To sound what stop she please. Give me that man
That is not passion's slave, and I will wear him
In my heart's core, aye, in my heart of heart,
As I do thee." (*Hamlet*, III, 2)

Much could be written, no doubt, on comparisons between the two princes, Arjuna and Hamlet - of their nobility, their moral dilemma, their doubt and hesitation and their final resort to action. Suffice it, however, to draw a few parallels between Shakespeare's play and the *Gītā* which suggest that a form of Advaita philosophy somehow reached the Elizabethan theatre.

Most obvious of all is Polonius' advice to his son, in which a foolish old man betrays a gleam of wisdom:

"This above all - to thine own self be true,
And it must follow, as the night the day,
Thou canst not then be false to any man."

(ibid. I, 3)

In the most famous soliloquy of Hamlet there are several references to sleep and dreams which imply that the real question is not one of suicide, or even of action against King Claudius, so much as whether to awake and see things in the light of reason or to fall back into the twilight world of dreams and the oblivion of sleep. Is reason, capable of looking before and after, "to fust in us unus'd", or to be elicited as a prime weapon against ignorance and indolence, as it was for Arjuna? Later, Hamlet refers to the play performed at Elsinore as holding the mirror up to nature, a comprehensive view of nature akin to that given in Chapter VII of the *Gītā*, where everything from earth to ego is included. The Sanskrit word "buddhi"[29], meaning intellect, conveys the idea of reflecting all that is experienced, like the playwright envisaged - and demonstrated - by Shakespeare. Finally, when Laertes is dying, he calls to Hamlet, "Mine and my father's death come not upon thee, nor thine on me![30]", as though he recognizes the truth that Kṛṣṇa impresses upon Arjuna that the Self is not killed and does not kill. The subject and object of killing are both no more than forces of nature. All these are but hints, contained in one play, that the philosophy of the *Gītā* is close to the philosophy of William Shakespeare. No doubt there are many more in the other plays.

An explanation of this influence upon Shakespeare is suggested by the fact that if the *Gītā* is read without any preconceptions about its provenance in India or its influence upon the Hindu religion, it can be seen as conveying a teaching remarkably similar to that of Jesus as presented in the Gospels. Jesus insisted on the unity of God:

> "And Jesus answered him, The first of all the commandments is, Hear, O Israel; The Lord our God is one Lord."
>
> (Mark, 12, 29)

and the Church has never forgotten this unity, however much the doctrine of the Trinity has made it difficult to expound:

> "And the Catholick Faith is this: That we worship one God in Trinity, and Trinity in Unity;
> Neither confounding the Persons: nor dividing the Substance.

---

29. See Note on *Buddhi*.

30. *Hamlet*, V, 2.

For there is one Person of the Father, another
of the Son: and another of the Holy Ghost.
But the Godhead of the Father, of the Son
and of the Holy Ghost, is all one."

(The Creed of Saint Anathasius)

The one substance is not to be divided, for it is that one Self common to all states of consciousness, eternally present and the ground of all experience. This teaching of Advaita at the root of the Christian and Hindu religions - and perhaps of all others - is what Jesus and Kṛṣṇa came into the world to propound. Both were incarnations (avatāras)[31] who took upon themselves the task of revitalizing the world at a time of degeneration - the function of an avatāra at whatever time, and in whatever form, he appears:

"O Bhārata, when law is in decline
And irreligion in ascendancy,
I am incarnate here upon this earth.
To save good men, annihilate the bad,
To see that dharma is observed once more,
I am begotten here in every age."

(IV, 7-8)

Kṛṣṇa does not see Himself as different from any other incarnation; He knows that He is the same Self that is embodied in all incarnations. Thus, from the standpoint of Advaita, when Kṛṣṇa or Jesus say "I", they refer to the same I, the one Self of all. Moreover, this Self (Ātman)[32] is the same as the universal Spirit (Brahman), just as the

31. 'Avatāra' means 'descent', but in particular the descent of a deity to earth. The first avatāra is said to have appeared in the Silver Age, since in the Golden Age an incarnation was not needed. Rāma was a Silver Age avatāra, Kṛṣṇa of the Bronze Age, and Christ may be regarded as the avatāra of the Iron Age.

32. See Note on *Ātman*

Son, Christ, is the same as the Father. On the one hand, the Gospel of St. John continually reaffirms the identity of Father and Son; on the other, the *Gītā*, more explicitly, elaborates upon the identity of Kṛṣṇa, as the immanent Spirit in the world, with Brahman, so that Arjuna, amazed at the vision of Kṛṣṇa's universal form, cries out:

"All hail to you! Great Father, hail, hail, hail!
A thousand salutations, hail to you!
In front, behind, on every side, all hail,
O Absolute, O infinite in power,
O Lord of valour, immanent in all."

(XI, 39-40)

Just as Christ proclaimed Himself the beginning and the end of all things[33], so too does Kṛṣṇa:

"I am the Ātman in the hearts of all;
Of beings the beginning, life and end."

(X, 20)

As the Creator of the world, Christ is the source of time, as the angel in Revelations comprehended in swearing "that there should be time no longer"[34]. Kṛṣṇa, as Creator and Destroyer, assumes the form of time itself:

"I am that Time which overturns the world;
Which, even now, destroys all creatures here."

(XI, 32)

Above all, Kṛṣṇa, like Jesus Christ, is the redeemer of mankind. Through His teaching men may find the truth about themselves and the created world; through His compassion they may find eternal peace in the Godhead, the source of all. The worst of sinful men may yet cross the sea of evil deeds by hearing the wisdom spoken by Kṛṣṇa [35]:

---

33. *Revelations*, I, 8; XXI, 6; XXII, 13

34. *ibid*, X, 6

35. *Gītā*, IV, 36

"This I promise you,
For you are dear to me. Abandoning
All actions, good and bad, in Me alone
Seek refuge; do not grieve, and I Myself,
O Bhārata, will free you from all sin."

(XVIII, 66)

Though presented in the sacrificial doctrine of Christian theology, the teaching given by Christ is the same: that the wisdom of the incarnation frees all who hear it from sin:

"But if we walk in the light, as he is in the light,
we have fellowship one with another, and the
blood of Jesus Christ his Son cleanseth us from all sin."

(I John, I, 7)

To seek refuge in Kṛṣṇa, to seek refuge in Christ, is onc and the same; for when the incarnation speaks of Himself he means the Ātman, the One Self which dwells in the hearts of all. In that Self, in the I that creates, sustains and dissolves all experience but never itself passes away, lies reality. The message of the *Song of the Lord* is to remember that truth.

Brian Hodgkinson

THE
BHAGAVAD GĪTĀ

Chapter 1
The Grief of Arjuna

On Kurukṣetra's sacred field were met 1
The King Yudhiṣṭhira's Pāṇḍava host,
With their own cousins of the Kuru clan,
The mighty Dhṛtarāṣṭra's vengeful sons,
Confronting one another, keen to fight.
When King Duryodhana, the eldest son 2
Of Dhṛtarāṣṭra, saw the Pāṇḍu force,
To his own teacher, Droṇa, lord of arms,
He turned and cried aloud these fearful words:
"Behold, O Master, this Pāṇḍava host, 3
Led by Drupada's son whom you have taught,
Heroic men, though enemies of ours, 4
All mighty archers, equal in their strength
To Arjuna and Bhīma, brothers royal.
There, too, stands Drupada the charioteer,
Virāta, Yuyudhāna and the king
Of distant Kāshi, with Dṛshṭaketu 5
Chekitāna, Kuntibhoja, Purujit,
Heroic Yudhāmanyu, and Shaibya, 6
Famous, indeed, in war, and Saubhadrā,
And then the valiant Uttamaujas too,

And all the fearsome sons of Draupadī:
Each one a match for thousands of their foes.
Peace-loving Master, twice-born *brāhmaṇa**, 7
Hear also of the men who lead my troops.
You Master are the first, and then Bhīṣma, 8
Then Karṇa, then victorious Kṛpa,
Your brother-in-law who stands beside you now,
Aśvattāma and Vikarṇa too,
And Jayadratha, Somadatta's son,
And then so many battle-hardened men, 9
Armed with all kinds of weapons, ready now,
To give their lives for me. Yet still these men, 10
So countless as they wait Bhīṣma's command,
Seem quite unwieldy, to my own dismay,
In facing Bhīma's strong, compact array."

Then Duryodhana stood and shouted out: 11
"Stand firm; support brave Bhīṣma in the field,
Stay at your posts till all Pāṇḍavas yield."

At this, Bhīṣma himself, aged yet strong, 12
Eldest of all the Kuru clan, roared forth,
Lionlike, and sounded his huge conch
To stir the heart of King Duryodhana.
To this the assembled Kurus gave support, 13
A mighty clamour, shrill with conch-shell horns,
With trumpets and the steady tabor's beat,
And multitudes of booming, heavy drums.

A swift reply the Pāṇḍu leaders made: 14
Kṛṣṇa himself and Arjuna arose
To stand unmoving in their gilded car,
Yoked with white horses; and then, as one,
They blew their conches, instruments of gods,
Pāñchajanya and Devadatta both. 15
Then Bhīma, too, whose very name spread fear,
Put to his lips the massive Pauṇḍra conch;
King Yudhiṣṭhira, son of Queen Kuntī, 16
On Anantavijaya blew aloud;
Whilst Nakula and Sahadeva too
Raised high their shrill and glittering horns.
From many more the same note pierced the sky: 17
From Śikhaṇḍi, and from the archer king
Of Kāśi, from Dhṛṣṭadyumna, Drupada,
Virāṭa, and invincible Sātyaki,
From sons of Draupadī, and mighty-armed
The son of Saubhadra; till every heart 19
Of Kauravas was rent by that huge noise
That shook the earth, resounded in the sky.
Arjuna bravely then took up his bow 20
Below his monkey's ensign, reason's mark;
Clearly he saw King Dhṛtarāṣṭra's troops
Preparing for the hail of deadly shafts.
He cried aloud to Kṛṣṇa, Lord of All: 21
"O steadfast Lord, drive forth my car of war
Between these hostile ranks, whence I may see 22
Opposing armies eager to engage.
In this brief moment, whilst the onslaught waits,

Let me behold these men whom I must fight, 23
These gathered here for Dhṛtarāṣṭra's son,
To die for him, despite what he has done."

Swiftly the Lord Śrī Kṛṣṇa drove ahead 24
To place their chariot, finest of them all,
Between each army, facing every king 25
Who followed Bhīṣma, those on Droṇa's side.
"O Prince!" he said, "look on this noble sight,
The whole Kaurava family come to fight."

Grandfathers stood there, uncles, brothers, sons, 26
Grandsons and teachers, friends and allies too.
On seeing them on every side aligned, 27
Heart-rending sorrow overcame the Prince:
"O Kṛṣṇa!" he cried out in bitter voice, 28
"To see my noble kinsmen waiting here,
Intent upon so cruel a war as this,
Unstrings my limbs and turns my mouth to dust;
My body shakes, my skin is pricked with fear. 29
My bow, Gāṇḍīva, quits my lifeless hand
And with despair my flesh itself burns dry.
O Kṛṣṇa, you who slay the fiend Keśi, 30
I can no longer stand; my mind gives way.
Omens, I see, of grim and sure import.
What good can come of slaying my own kin? 31
I seek no victory, nor empire's pride,
Nor the vain pleasures of the turning world.

What use is sovereign power, O Lord of All? 32
What use are riches, what use life itself,
When those for whom we want these spoils of war
Stand ready, they themselves, to join the fray, 33
Renouncing all alike the breath of life:
These men, our teachers, fathers and our sons, 34
Grandfathers, grandsons, uncles, kinsmen all;
The fathers, brothers, too, of our dear wives?
Though they kill me, I have no wish to strike 35
Such men as these; O Kṛṣṇa, not indeed
To gain the triple world, still less this earth.
O slayer of Jana, how could we rest, 36
If once the blood of Dhṛtarāṣṭra's sons
Stained our pale hands? Their crimes would cling.
Killing of kin must ever be condemned. 37
Slayer of Madhu, when they lie there dead
Where do we turn to find our true content?
Decay of family, treachery to friends, 38
They cannot see, whom greed has rendered blind.
Can we, who know this law, ignore the crime? 39
When families fall their ancient rites are lost 40
And, losing sight of law, they are destroyed
By lack of righteousness. Unfaithful then 41
Are women to their lords and, once corrupt,
Give birth to tainted castes, which soon commits
Them all to hell on earth. O noble Lord, 42
O Kṛṣṇa of the mighty Vṛṣṇi clan,
Then wane the ancient spirits of the kin,
Deprived of food and sacred water gifts.

By this offence 'gainst purity of caste 43
Eternal law itself, the one *dharma**
Of caste and kin, is wholly broken down.
Then is it said that once bereft of law 44
A family lives in hell, Janārdana.
Alas, we are resolved on this great crime, 45
To murder kindred for the greed of power.
Were Dhṛtarāṣṭra's sons to cut me down, 46
To slay me whilst I stood without my sword,
Declining in the midst of war to fight,
I should be better served, better in right."

Thus Arjuna cried out, poised in between 47
The massive armies waiting to deploy
On Kurukṣetra's sacred battlefield.
With bitter grief he cast away his bow
And sank upon his chariot's gilded chair,
His mind o'erwhelmed by sorrow and despair.

Chapter 2
The Way of Reason

Arjuna lay, dejected, full of grief, 1
Unseeing through his eyes bedimmed with tears,
Until the Lord, the slayer of Madhu,
Majestic Kṛṣṇa, roused him with these words:
"Whence comes such frailty, noble-minded lord, 2
Which closes fast the welcome gates of heaven
And swiftly brings disgrace? Shun impotence, 3
O worthy Pṛthā's son; it suits you ill.
Cast feebleness away, forget your woes,
And with the fire of valour scorch your foes."

Arjuna then replied: "O demon-slayer, 4
How can I shoot my arrows of sure aim
At Bhīṣhma, Droṇa and their noble peers,
These worthy men to whom all honour's due?
Better by far a beggar here and now 5
Than soon to kill these great and holy lords;
For all the wealth, whatever I desire,
Would turn to worldly pleasures stained with blood
Were I to kill them. Which is the just event, 6
That they are vanquished or they vanquish us?
These mighty sons of Dhṛtarāṣṭra there

Who face us now arrayed upon the plain,
Were we to slay them would we should not live!
Consuming pity lacerates my heart 7
And duty hides in deep obscurity.
Tell me, I do implore, dear Lord, what is
For certain best. Instruct me now in this.
I am your pupil, who has sought your grace.
Nothing I see to cool this burning grief 8
Which withers every sense; not mastery
Of earth, nor lordship of the gods themselves."
Then finally that invincible warrior cried: 9
"I shall not fight," and sank upon the field.

The blessed Lord Śrī Kṛṣṇa gently smiled: 10
"You speak with some intelligence, yet grieve. 11
What right can sorrow claim? The wise grieve not;
In life and death they find no cause to mourn.
There never was a time when I was not, 12
Nor when these kings, and you, did not exist,
Nor shall there be a time when we have ceased.
A single body passes through each age 13
As men grow old; so does the Spirit pass
Through cycles of these brief embodiments.
Wise men are not disturbed by such events.
O son of Kuntī, bear all things of sense; 14
They are impermanent; they rise and fall.
Bear heat and cold, sweet pleasure and dire pain,
Born from mere touch of objects with their sense.
Be worthy of the kin of Bharata!

That steady man unshaken by these trials, 15
For whom such fleeting moments are the same,
Proves fit indeed for immortality.
What is not real does not in fact exist; 16
That which is real exists eternally:
Who knows this difference sees the final truth.
Time cannot move the substance of all things; 17
Immutable, it cannot be destroyed.
Though bodies end, this Self shall never change; 18
It lives for ever, boundless in its scope.
O valiant scion of your race, fight on!
Who thinks the Self may kill, who thinks the Self 19
Itself be killed, has missed the mark of truth.
Self is not born, nor does it ever die; 20
It does not come to life, not having been,
Nor, having been, does it thereafter cease.
Eternal, ancient, ever-present Self,
Though bodies are cut down, lives on intact.
O son of gentle Pṛthā, how can men 21
Who know this unborn Self will never change
In all eternity, how can they kill
Or seem to cause another so to do?
As old clothes are cast off for sake of new, 22
So too are worn-out bodies left aside
By Man's undying Soul. Not edge of sword, 23
Nor fire, nor fury of the wind, nor rain,
Touch that pure substance which pervades them all. 24
Beyond perception and the range of thought 25
The undivided Spirit stands, unchanged.
Know this and do not grieve, courageous lord.

For even if you think that Spirit's born 26
And later dies, in never ending turn,
Why therefore grieve at what no-one avoids?
For what may die awaits to be reborn, 27
Whatever may be born is sure to die.
You merely see brief intervals between 28
All creatures' births and deaths. What cause for grief?
A few men look with wonder on the Self; 29
A few more, full of wonder, speak of it;
Whilst others hear of it as wonderful.
But who, of these, can truly comprehend?
That Self in every creature is not killed, 30
So do not grieve, O kin of Bharata.
Why tremble when you merely see that law 31
Of your own nature as a lord of men?
No field of action suits a soldier more
Than fighting in a war for what is just;
For such a battle opens heaven's gates 32
And warriors rejoice to enter there.
If you evade this righteous course of war 33
And lay aside your duty and renown,
Then sin will mark you. Ever will men speak 34
Of your dishonour, hated more than death
By any soldier worthy of esteem.
All in this army here will think you quit 35
The Kurukṣetra field from craven fear,
A man of no account who once was great,
Whose enemies will talk with foul contempt, 36
Belittling all your powers. What could be worse?

Yet once struck down upon this sacred field, 37
The hosts of heaven will proclaim you great,
Or, once victorious here, you will command
The earth itself. So stand resolved to fight,
O noble Kunī's son, heedless of pain, 38
Not caring overmuch which side shall win,
And casting from you every charge of crime.
Thus have I taught how reason may destroy 39
That bond of evil, ignorance of Self.
But now, O Pārtha, hear the *yogin's** way
Which breaks apart the fetters of past lives.
No effort made in yoga can be lost. 40
From *yoga* nothing evil can ensue;
It soon dissolves the terror of rebirth.
O son of Kuru, *yogins* hold one thought 41
Whilst inattentive men turn every way,
Their thoughts like endless branches of a tree.
The ignorant, irresolute of mind, 42-44
Attached to pleasure and pursuit of power,
Are soon misled by those of florid words,
Who search the *Veda** for its praise of gods
And, full of lust, want heaven for themselves.
Their speech extols the means to worldly ends,
In promising rebirth, and nothing else.
O son of Pṛthā, *Vedic* rites refer 45
To three *guṇas** which hold this world in thrall.
Rise up, O noble lord, transcend these bonds,
Cast off the thought of pairs of opposites,
Of getting and preserving, and hold fast
To simple goodness and to your own Self.

What use have men who live in wisdom's flood 46
For meagre drops of ritualistic lore?
You have the right to work, to that alone, 47
To any fruits you have no claim at all,
So let all hope of benefit be gone -
And yet beware the love of indolence.
As one who wins the accolades of praise 48
On every side, O Arjuna, stand firm,
Intent upon your work, yet unattached,
And quite the same in failure and success;
For that is *yoga*, evenness of mind.
In reason seek your refuge, mighty lord, 49
For then one no more acts from mere desire.
Who seeks results leads but a wretched life.
Devote yourself instead to *yoga's* art, 50
Which soon dissolves the binding power of work,
And take no thought for actions, good or bad.
Intelligent men, with temperance of mind, 51
Indifferent to effects of any act,
Escape for ever cycles of rebirth,
And find themselves an uncorrupted place.
When your mind likewise is no more confused, 52
You will ignore the multitude of words
Heard in the past and still to be endured.
Free from perplexity, your mind shall stay 53
Within your Self, untroubled by the past;
There you will rest, one with your Self, at last."

Then Arjuna enquired, "That man of truth 54
Who contemplates the Self, what is he like?
How does he sit? How does he move and speak?"

"O son of Kuntī," Kṛṣṇa answered him, 55
"Who gives up all desire and rests content
In his own Self with that same Self alone,
Is said to be a man who truly knows.
Adversity does not unsettle him, 56
Nor does he long for comfort, nor for love.
He stands unmoved by fear or passing rage;
And thus he earns the epithet of wise.
Good fortune finds no welcome at his hands, 57
Nor does he hate the crueller blows of time,
But, as a tortoise draws its limbs within, 58
So does he free his senses from the world.
With ease are sensual pleasures all forgone 59
By any abstinent man, but not their taste;
That only fades for him who knows the Self.
O son of Kuntī, senses overbear 60
With heedless turbulence the minds of men
Who strive in earnest for control of mind;
But one who sits, his senses well restrained, 61
Steadfast in knowledge, quite intent on Me,
Is firm in wisdom, with all sense subdued.
If any man dwells long on sensual forms, 62
Attachment surely comes; from this, desire,
Which soon engenders rage; and after rage
The loss of right and wrong; and from this loss 63
All memory of the sacred teaching fails;

So reason dies from loss of memory,
And reason dead, there perishes the man.
But he whose inner life is self-controlled, 64
Who moves, with senses yoked, amongst all things,
Without aversion, nor with appetite,
Attains a peace where sorrow has no place, 65
For reason has a sure foundation there.
Unsteadiness destroys the power to know, 66
And then to meditate, and hence the way
To that same peace which meditation brings.
What happiness remains devoid of that?
For wayward senses draw the mind off course, 67
Like ships by veering wind; and with it goes
Discrimination's power. Yet who restrains 68
Each from their object, every wilful sense,
His knowledge is most firm, O Arjuna.
For such a one, what all men call the night 69
Is when he wakes; whilst when they wake is what
He calls the night. There is no peace for him 70
Who wants desire, but when, as rivers flow
And fill the tranquil ocean from all sides,
Desires flow into him, that man finds peace,
Longing for nothing, giving up desire, 71
Without a sense of "I" or what is "mine";
O son of Pṛthā, that is peace indeed.
He is no more deluded who comes there; 72
It is to find the *Brahman** here on earth.
For such a man is final bliss revealed,
Even in death, even upon this field."

Chapter 3
The Way of Action

Once more Arjuna asked the Lord of All, 1
"If then to know is greater than to act,
What should impel me to this dreadful deed?
Bewilderment at your conflicting words 2
Confuses now my mind. Tell me, I pray,
How I may find the truth, the certain way."

The Blessed Lord replied, "O sinless one, 3
My words, when all began, gave to this world
A twofold path beloved of devotees:
The way of knowledge first, then action's way.
Freedom from action never shall be found 4
By mere inaction, nor shall renouncing
Bring men to that end; for in each moment 5
Actions are performed. All men are helpless,
Driven on to act by those three *guṇas*
Which pervade the world; and those who curb 6
Their outward acts alone are hypocrites,
Who dwell within intent on sensual lust,
Deluded by themselves; esteemed the more 7
That man, quite unattached, whose mind controls
The wanderings of sense, although he acts.

Whatever is your duty, follow that, 8
For action is superior to sloth
And even your own body needs support;
And yet, O son of Kuntī, always make 9
Your every action as a sacrifice
In freedom from all worldly interests,
For men are bound, except by sacrifice.
*Brahmā** created sacrifice itself 10
Within the very act of making man.
Of sacrifice he spoke these holy words:
'By sacrifice alone you will bear fruit;
This cow of plenty quenches every thirst;
The gods, so nourished, nourish you in turn 11
And you shall then attain the highest good.
Whatever you desire, the gods will give.' 12
But he who takes what gifts the gods may make,
Yet offers nothing to them in return,
That man indeed is verily a thief.
When sacrifice is made, all righteous men 13
Eat what is left and free themselves from sin;
Unrighteous men, who offer nothing back,
In lack of sacrifice feed on their sin.
From food all living creatures first arise, 14
From rain comes food, from sacrifice comes rain,
From action sacrifice, from *Veda* action. 15
For there within the heart of sacrifice
The all-pervading *Veda* takes its stand,
Begotten from the one unmoved *Brahman*.
A sinful man who quits this sacrifice, 16
The wheel that turns upon the *Veda's* hub,

Indulging thus in sensual appetite,
Lives here in vain, O noble Pṛthā's son;
But who alone rejoices in the Self, 17
Contented with himself, at peace within,
Though he may act, has nothing left to do.
He has no end to yearn for in this world, 18
No object which he needs from anyone.
Whatever action ought to be performed, 19
Do that, Arjuna, free from any claims;
This path for certain reaches the Supreme.
King Janaka and others sought the good 20
In action only; so then should you act,
In looking to the welfare of the world.
Men follow what the greatest men perform, 21
Taking their standards from the hero's wonts.
O son of Pṛthā, not in these three worlds 22
Am I obliged to act, for nought remains
For Me to undertake; and yet I act.
Were I to cease from My unwearied work 23
All men would follow such an idle path.
From Me would stem confusion of the castes, 24
The worlds would soon decay and creatures die.
Whilst fools forever act for selfish ends,
Wise men, though also acting, stay unbound, 25
Intent upon the care of all mankind.
They do not stir the ignorant to doubt, 26
Who seek results, but through their steadiness
Encourage others to act thus themselves.

"I am the doer" thinks the foolish man, 27
Deluded by an image of himself,
Not knowing that the *guṇas* act alone;
Whilst yet, O mighty-armed, a man of sight 28
Discerns the *guṇas* and the acts they cause
And, staying unattached, lets senses move
Amidst their ends, the fivefold elements.
He does not then disturb dull-witted men 29
Bemused by how the *guṇas* operate,
Who are attached to what the *guṇas* do.
With mind intent upon the Self alone, 30
Renouncing hope, regardless of yourself,
To none but Me now dedicate your work,
And fight in earnest, casting off your grief.
Who practises this teaching undeterred, 31
Without complaint and ever filled with trust,
He is no longer bound by what he does,
But whosoever murmurs at My words 32
And fails to practise this philosophy,
From such a man all knowledge is concealed,
And thus deprived, his ruin is assured.
Each being's nature is the law for it, 33
Even for those who know. What good constraint?
Within the senses nature has ordained 34
Attraction and aversion for all things;
Avoid their force; they are your enemies.
Perform your duty, though imperfectly; 35
Not another's, howsoever well,
For pregnant with disaster is that course.

Better to die in doing what you ought,
Than live another's life which comes to nought."

At this, Arjuna asked, "O Varṣṇeya, 36
What makes a man descend, as though compelled,
To sinful acts, his proper will withheld?"

To this response the Blessed Lord replied, 37
"Driven by *rajas*, it is man's desire,
His anger, all-consuming, full of sin.
Here in this world your enemy is that.
As smoke obscures the sacrificial fire, 38
As dust hides mirrors, or as embryos
Lie long concealed within the mother's womb,
So, by desire, is knowledge cloaked from view.
O son of Kuntī, this confronts the wise, 39
Their constant and their unrelenting foe.
It dwells in intellect, in mind and sense, 40
Obscuring knowledge for embodied men.
Curb senses first, O bull of Bhāratas; 41
Then kill this evil thing which soon destroys
All knowledge, both in principle and use.
Though senses are the master of the flesh, 42
Discursive mind, in turn, the lord of sense,
Intelligence the ruler, next, of mind,
Beyond all these, O mighty-armed, is He.
Conquer yourself with Him, and never tire 43
To kill that stubborn enemy, desire."

Chapter 4
Renunciation through Action

The Blessed Lord then said, "To Vivasvat 1
I gave this *yoga*, free from time's decay;
He taught it then to Manu, who in turn
Taught King Ikṣvāku, first *Kṣatriya*.
To every mighty ruler it descends, 2
Until within the long expanse of time
It seems to perish. Yet, O Pārtha, you, 3
Amongst all men, have heard these ancient words,
This deepest secret, most profound of all,
Offered to you, this very day, by Me,
O scourge of foes, My friend and devotee."

Then Arjuna enquired, "Was not your birth 4
Later than Vivasvat's, O mighty Lord?
How then in the beginning came your word?"

To Arjuna the Blessed Lord replied, 5
"Numerous births we have both undergone,
But I remember all, whilst you forget.
Though never born, in nature never changed, 6
Lord of all creatures, yet I seem to live
In My own dream, My nature overruled.

O Bhārata, when law is in decline 7
And irreligion in ascendancy,
I am incarnate here upon this earth.
To save the good, annihilate the bad, 8
To see that *dharma* is observed once more,
I am begotten here in every age.
Whoever, then, acknowledges this truth 9
About My incarnation in the world,
He is not born again, but comes to Me.
For freed from passion, freed from fear and rage, 10
By fire of knowledge purified in heart,
Identified with Me, their safe retreat,
So many have at last attained to Me.
But though, O Pārtha, all men follow Me, 11
The form they seek determines their reward.
Thus in the world, where ends are soon achieved,
The gods are worshipped by ambitious men, 12
Who want success from every kind of act.
I long ago established human castes, 13
Dividing men by guṇas and by acts
Into four kinds; and yet though author of
These various castes, I do not act
But stay immutable. I am not touched 14
By actions, nor seek fruits. Who knows me so,
However he may act, remains unbound.
The ancient sages sought for freedom thus, 15
So imitate your kin, O Bhārata.
Action? Inaction? What in truth are these? 16
This problem makes the wise themselves draw back,

But I shall teach you what they really are,
And, knowing that, you will be free from sin.
You must enquire what lawful action is, 17
Even the nature of inaction too,
For action is most hard to understand.
That man is wise who sees in every act 18
Inaction hidden; who sees inaction
As a form of act. He is a *yogin*,
Mastering what is done. For such as he
The fire of knowledge burns away desire; 19
His acts are purposeless, devoid of plan.
How can he want the fruits - he is content? 20
Upon himself alone the sage depends,
In doing nothing yet engaged in acts.
Without possessions and beyond desire, 21
And in command of body and the mind,
He meets his earthly needs and does not sin.
With what he may receive from time to time 22
He is well pleased. Beyond dislike and like,
Beyond all envy and of even mind,
He is not bound by failure and success,
Although he acts. He is no more attached, 23
But firm in knowledge, finally released.
His acts and their effects no more exist
And work is done for sacrifice alone.
The one eternal Spirit is the gift, 24
The *Brahman* sacrificed in His own fire
By *Brahman* to Himself; for who, indeed,
Sees *Brahman* in each act attains *Brahman*.

And whilst some *yogins* sacrifice to gods, 25
Yet others offer Self by means of Self
Within the *Brahman's* sacrificial fire,
Or in the fire restrain their every sense, 26
Or offer objects in perception's fire,
Or sacrifice the body's vital breaths 27
In that pure fire of *yoga*, self-control,
Which wisdom kindles. Some may offer wealth 28
And some austerity, whilst some withdraw
The mind, in *yoga*, from external things;
Whilst those of strictest vows make sacrifice
Of study and what knowledge they acquire.
Yet others, practising restraint of breath, 29
Offer the outward in the inward one,
Inward in outward, stopping each in turn;
And those of measured diet sacrifice 30
The other vital breaths in that one breath
Which they control. These men of sacrifice,
By sacrifice, wipe out their evil deeds
And feast on nectar of eternal life 31
By eating just what sacrifice has left,
And hence return to *Brahman*. But who oft
Refuses sacrifice, this world rejects;
How then another world, O best Kuru?
From *Vedic* teaching sacrifice is learnt; 32
Its origin is action, not the Self;
In knowing this you will be truly free.
And better than the sacrifice of things 33
Is sacrifice of knowledge, O Pārtha,
For knowledge is the source of every act.

Scorcher of foes, fall down before the wise, 34
Enquire of them, attend upon their needs,
For then this knowledge will be freely taught.
O Pāṇḍava, no more deluded then, 35
You will perceive all beings in yourself,
And hence within Me also. Were you still 36
The worst of sinful men, yet would you cross
The sea of evil deeds on wisdom's boat;
For just as blazing fire turns wood to ash, 37
So knowledge burns away an act's effect.
Nothing in this world so purifies. 38
Whoever's freed by *yoga* finds, in time,
This knowledge for himself within Himself.
He who devotes himself to wisdom's cause, 39
Restrains his senses, and is full of faith,
Attains that wisdom and, soon after, peace;
But ignorant and faithless men are lost; 40
More so the man who will forever doubt:
Not this world even, nor the joys of heaven,
Nor any happiness, may he expect.
Dhanañjaya, no actions fetter men 41
Whose doubts are split asunder by the truth,
Who have renounced by yoga every act,
And come to rest in self-sufficiency.
Raise the sharp sword of knowledge to your heart, 42
Cut out this anxious doubt about the Self,
Resort to *yoga*, armour of the wise,
Fight on, O Bhārata, fight on, arise!"

Chapter 5
The Way of Renunciation

Arjuna then replied to Kṛṣṇa's words, 1
"You praise renouncing action, and yet praise
Performance of it too. How is this so?
Tell me, O Kṛṣṇa, Lord of all the earth,
Has action, or inaction, greater worth?

The Blessed Lord then said to Arjuna, 2
"Both these are ways which lead to final bliss,
And yet far better to perform an act
Than merely to renounce it outwardly.
He who renounces truly every act, 3
Neither dislikes nor likes, nor is he touched
By pleasure, pain and other opposites;
From bondage he is easily set free.
O mighty Arjuna, it is but fools 4
Who talk of renunciation as distinct
From acts performed devoted to Myself;
He truly sees who sees these as the same. 5
Who follows either gains the fruit of both;
They lead to one same state, though to renounce 6
Is hard indeed without devoted acts.

Absorbed in *yoga*, rid of all self-will, 7
Cleansed of impurity, controlled in sense,
Himself become the Self of all the world,
A sage, through *yoga*, reaches the Supreme:
He is not tainted, though he seems to act.
Steadfast in action, he thinks "I do not act", 8
In seeing, hearing, touching, smell or taste,
In moving, sleeping, breathing in or out,
In taking and in giving, and in speech, 9
Or even in the closing of the eyes,
He is aware that senses merely move
Amongst their objects. Thus quite unattached,
He offers *Brahman* everything he does.
From every taint of sin he lives immune, 10
Like lotus leaves upon the water's brim.
With this indifference *yogins* carry out 11
All actions of the body, senses, mind,
And even those of reason, with one aim,
To purify themselves, and that alone.
Unsteady men, who follow their desires, 12
Cling to the fruit of action and are bound,
Whilst he who lives, abandoning rewards,
By his devotion finds eternal peace.
Within himself renouncing every act, 13
He rests in happiness, all senses quelled,
At home within the city of nine gates,
Devoid of action, causing none to act.
The Lord creates no agency, nor acts, 14
Nor does He join the agent to an end;
All these effects have nature as their cause.

He takes account of no-one, good or bad. 15
For ignorance alone obscures the truth
And thereby mortal beings are misled.
When, however, knowledge of the Self 16
Shines on that darkness like the Sun itself,
Unwisdom goes and *Brahman* is revealed.
And they whose Self is that, intent on that, 17
With intellect absorbed in that alone,
With life devoted to that final end,
They go beyond return; and from such men
By wisdom are their sins all cast away.
In *brahmins*, full of knowledge without pride, 18
In cows and elephants, and even dogs,
And even in the outcast who eats dogs,
These men of wisdom look upon the same.
Who rests his mind in that equality 19
Transcends this earthly life, and therefore lives
In that *Brahman* who likewise is the same,
In whom no kind of imperfection dwells.
He does not greet the pleasant with delight, 20
Nor painful things with grief. He rests in that,
Without delusion and with steady mind;
And, unattached to objects in the world 21
He realises the joy within the Self.
Then, deep in contemplation of *Brahman*,
He comes, indeed, to everlasting bliss.
Those pleasures born of contact with the world, 22
Begin and end; they are the source of pain.
In these, O Prince, the wise do not rejoice.

Who then withstands, before his body falls, 23
Impulsive claims of anger and desire
Is truly steadfast and a happy man.
A *yogin* finds within himself his joy, 24
His place of rest, the light by which he lives,
Himself becomes *Brahman*, attains His bliss.
Rid of doubts and cleansed of every sin, 25
Resolved upon the welfare of the world,
The ṛṣis, also, masters of themselves,
Absorbed in *Brahman*, find their freedom there;
As do all devotees who know the Self, 26
Control the mind and give up all desire.
Once and for all they reach *nirvana** here.
He who abstains from all external touch 27
And centres all his sight between the eyes,
Through the nostrils measuring out his breath;
He who restrains the senses, mind and heart 28
And seeks for nothing else but to be free,
Abandoning desire and fear and wrath:
That ever constant sage is truly free.
He knows Me as the source of sacrifice, 29
The one from whom austerities arise;
He knows Me as the Lord of every world,
The friend of all, whose friendship shall not cease,
And, thus assured, he finds eternal peace."

Chapter 6
Meditation

Then said the Blessed Lord, "Who carries out 1
His proper duty with no thought at all
Of what the fruits will be, he is indeed
A *saṃnyāsin** and *yogin*, both of these,
Unlike that man who shuns fire sacrifice
Or fails to act when action is required.
Remember, son of Pāṇḍu, this advice: 2
Yoga is renunciation's name;
No one becomes a *yogin* verily
If he retain the thought of a result. 3
The way of action is for devotees
Who wish to practise *yoga*; though for those
Who are possessed already of its power,
To whom no things of sense, nor actions, cling, 4
Quiescence is the way; they have renounced
All images of gain. A man should raise 5
Himself by Himself only, his only
Friend Himself, and not demean himself
By his own Self, as though He were his foe.

To him who is the master of himself 6
The *Ātman** is a friend who helps him rise;
To him who lives at war within himself,
This *Ātman* is the foe who drags him down.
Within a man serene and disciplined, 7
The Spirit lives unmoved by heat or cold,
By pain or pleasure, honour or disgrace.
To such a one whom wisdom satisfies, 8
Who does not shake, whose senses are subdued,
A clod of earth, a stone, a piece of gold,
Are but the same to him; he is a saint.
Upon his friends, upon his enemies, 9
Upon impartial judges, or his kin,
Upon those full of hate, upon the good,
Upon both righteous and unrighteous men
He looks with equal eye, and by this means
Becomes pre-eminent. Let such a man, 10
With concentration of his powers within,
In quiet seclusion and with mind controlled,
Expecting nothing, nothing his to own,
Arrange himself a seat of skins and cloth, 11
On sacred grass at some befitting place,
And in the forest there sit down alone, 12
His mind and senses carefully restrained,
And meditate to purify the heart.
Seated securely, head and trunk erect, 13
And gazing, as it were, at his own nose,
Balanced, at peace, and free from any fear, 14
His vow confirmed to lead a blameless life,
Let him reflect upon Me as Supreme.

Such *yogins* reach My peace and thence proceed 15
To that *nirvana* which surpasses all.
O Arjuna, those men who eat too much, 16
Those who eat nothing, those who always sleep,
And even those who never sleep at all,
They cannot meditate; and yet for men 17
Whose lives are measured both in food and sleep,
Who judge the time when action is required,
This practice will destroy their misery.
With mind controlled and resting in the Self, 18
Not longing for the objects of desire,
Such devotees may be entitled saints.
Just as a lamp well sheltered from the wind, 19
Stands without flickering, so should one think
Of that firm *yogin*, disciplined in mind,
Who centres all his being in the Self.
For when his mind is silent, and he sees 20
The Self by means of self and rests content,
Knowing, beyond all sense, supreme delight, 21
And never moving from unmoving Self,
Not even dreadful pain can trouble him, 22
For that Reality he values most.
This severance from identity with pain 23
Is what is truly called the *yoga* state.
With perseverance practise to this end,
Downcast no more. Who puts desires aside
Without reserve, together with their aims, 24
And binds the senses fast on every side,
With intellect held firm, he comes to rest, 25
Keeping his mind intent upon the Self,

Thinking of nothing; but, if then the mind 26
Should wander needlessly, he leads it back,
Towards the jurisdiction of the Self.
The highest bliss awaits that taintless man 27
Whose passions are subdued, of peaceful mind,
For whom all things are *Brahman* and nought else.
No longer is it hard for him to find 28
The perfect joy of union with that.
He sees the same wherever he may look; 29
Beholds Myself abiding in all things
And yet all things abiding in Myself.
Who looks on Me whichever way he turns 30
And sees that every creature lives in Me,
Will never leave My presence, nor I his;
For whosoever is intent on One,
And whosoever worships Me alone 31
As Spirit of all beings, lives in Me,
Whatever mode of life he may select.
Who judges that all pleasure and all pain 32
Are in himself the same as in the rest,
He, of all the *yogins*, is the best."

"O slayer of Madhu!" Arjuna cried, 33
"Sooner harness the tempestuous wind
Than with the steady *yoga* you commend
Restrain for long the restless, forceful mind, 34
So turbulent, so quick, so unconfined!"

The Blessed Lord replied, "O mighty-armed, 35
Doubtless the wavering mind is hard to check.

Practice and indifference are the means,
O son of Kuntī, to restrain its force.
For one who lacks all sense of discipline 36
This *yoga* is impossible indeed,
But not for him whose discipline is strong,
Who seeks the proper way, however long."

"What hope remains," Arjuna then enquired, 37
"For one who wanders off from *yoga's* path
And yet has faith? What end shall he attain
If that perfection lies beyond his reach?
Is he to perish like a riven cloud 38
For failing to succeed in either course?
O mighty Kṛṣṇa! Has he no support,
Bewildered as he is about the way?
O Kṛṣṇa, rid me utterly of doubt; 39
No voice but yours may truly drive it out."

"Son of Pṛthā," the Blessed Lord replied, 40
"Not here and not hereafter does he die,
For men of goodwill meet no adverse fate.
Though having failed to follow *yoga's* path, 41
He reaches worlds where virtuous creatures dwell,
And after many years in that abode
He finds another pure and prosperous home,
Amongst a noble family here on earth,
Or even in a family of the wise, 42
Though such a birth is rare indeed to win.

Thus, meeting with that knowledge once again, 43
Derived from what he did in former lives,
He strives with greater ardour than before
For that perfection. O son of Kurus,
Still is he borne along, despite himself, 44
By all that he had practised earlier.
Even the mere desire to know has power
To carry men beyond all sacred rites.
And so, with constant striving, cleansed of sin, 45
Perfected by a multitude of births,
The truest *yogin* is assured his end.
He is esteemed beyond all other men: 46
Ascetics, thinkers, men of mighty deeds.
Be such a *yogin*, Arjuna, as this.
With heart absorbed entirely in Myself, 47
He worships Me alone, free from all doubt;
Amongst the righteous, he is most devout."

Chapter 7

Realisation through Knowledge

If you attend, O Pṛthā's son, to me, 1
And practise *"yoga"* said the Blessed Lord;
"If you seek refuge nowhere but in Me,
Then you will learn to know Me without doubt.
This knowledge with experience I give, 2
Which, if you hear, there is no more to know.
One, amongst thousands, strives for the Supreme, 3
Yet, of these few, but one knows Me in truth.
My lower nature has these eightfold parts: 4
Earth, water, fire, air, space and mental power,
Reason and ego; but, apart from this, 5
My higher nature, principle of life,
Sustains, O mighty-armed, this universe.
These double natures are all creatures' wombs, 6
And I Myself the source and death of all.
Nothing exists, Dhanañjaya, beyond; 7
For on Myself this universe is strung,
Like jewels, O son of Kuntī, on a thread.
I am, of limpid water, the sweet taste;

I am the radiance of Moon and Sun, 8
*OM** in all *Vedas*, and essential sound
Of space, and the humanity in men;
Pure scent in earth, and brilliant light of fire, 9
The life of every being and the zeal
Of those who undertake austerity.
Know Me as the eternal seed of all, 10
As *buddhi** of the wise, as bravery
Of heroes and, O Pārtha, as that strength 11
Which overcomes desire and is detached;
And in all men I am the one desire
Which follows *dharma*, Lord of Bhāratas.
Those beings which the threefold *guṇas* form, 12
That they arise in Me, be sure indeed,
For I am not in them, but they in Me.
Deluded by the *guṇas'* many shapes, 13
The world ignores Me, though I am beyond,
Distinct from them, the One immutable.
To cross beyond *māyā** is hard indeed - 14
My great illusion, godly in its scope -
For only those who seek Myself alone,
Shall come to Me upon the further side.
Those evil men, deluded and most vile, 15
Whose reason is misled by *māyā's* power,
Pursue the demons, rather than Myself.
Now I will tell you of four kinds of men, 16
Who worship Me as they are virtuous:
First the distressed, then those who look for wealth,
Then those who seek to know and, last, the wise.

Of these, the ever constant man, the sage, 17
Devoted to the One, excels them all;
I am most dear to him, and he to Me.
Noble, indeed, are all who worship Me, 18
But that wise man I deem My very Self,
For he makes Me his overriding goal,
And, firm in mind, resorts to Me alone.
So, after many births, he reaches Me, 19
Knowing that the inmost Self is all.
Such high nobility is rarely met.
But men whose power to choose is overborne 20
By this or that desire, engage in rites,
By their own natures led to other gods.
Whatever deities devout men seek, 21
I make their faith unshakeable, and thus,
In rendering homage to particular gods, 22
They satisfy desire through faithfulness,
Although it is Myself who makes it so.
Small-minded men reach what is limited, 23
And whoso worships gods, he goes to them,
But devotees of Mine attain to Me.
I am unmanifest, but fools believe 24
I have become a creature visible.
They are oblivious of My highest form,
Immutable and far beyond compare.
Veiled by *māyā*, I show Myself to few. 25
Unrecognised by this deluded world,
I am not born, nor shall I ever die.

Yet, Arjuna, I know these beings here, 26
Of past and present, others yet to come,
Though they do not know Me. O noble scion, 27
Scorcher of all foes, all creatures are
Deluded at their birth; for then aversion
And its pair, desire, create those opposites
Which cause *māyā*; yet even so some men, 28
Of virtuous deeds, no longer bound by sin
And freed from the delusion of *māyā*,
Hold fast in faith and come to worship Me.
They strive for freedom from old age and death, 29
Abandoning themselves to Me alone;
They know the Self in all, they know *Brahman*,
They know what action is. Within the worlds 30
Of creatures and of gods, within the world
Where sacrifice prevails, they find Me there.
At death itself, when life indeed has gone,
Steadfast in mind, they know Me, even then."

Chapter 8
The Imperishable Brahman

"What is that *Brahman*?" Arjuna then cried, 1
"And inmost Spirit, what indeed is that?
What, too, is action, *Puruṣottama**?
What is this thing we call material world,
And what is said to be the world of gods?
Who makes the sacrifice whilst in this world; 2
How is it done, O slayer of Madhu?
And how, when men of self-control face death,
May they, in spite of all, know you in truth?"

To these requests the Blessed Lord replied, 3
"What cannot die is *Brahman*, the Supreme,
And inmost Spirit is the very same,
Each person's one, imperishable Self.
Action is the offering which creates
The inner seed of every creature here.
What perishes is this material world; 4
The world of gods is where the Soul abides,
And I Myself am sacrifice on earth,
Inherent in the body, Arjuna.

So, at the time of death, whoever thinks 5
Of Me alone, in casting off his flesh,
Goes forth and comes to Me; there is no doubt.
For men attain that thing they dwell upon 6
At that brief moment when they leave this life,
Since that, O Kuntī, was their constant thought;
So now, and at all times, remember Me. 7
With mind unwavering on Me, then fight,
And you will come, assuredly, to Me.
For he, indeed, whose mind is not distraught, 8
But made steadfast by meditation's power,
Who dwells on shining Spirit, goes to that.
Who thinks of Me as ancient Lord of all, 9
Omniscient, sustainer of the world,
Smaller than atoms, and of form unknown,
Beyond all darkness, shining like the Sun,
Who at the time of death thus meditates,
With mind unmoved, imbued with *yoga's* force, 10
Holding the breath of life between his brows,
Attains to that supreme Divinity.
Now let Me speak in brief about that goal 11
Which sages call the undecaying end,
Approached by those who practise self-control
And, free from passion, lead a godly life.
Whoso withdraws his mind within the heart, 12-13
Closes the gates of sense, and in his head,
Firm in *yoga*, holds life-giving breath,
With *Brahman's* name of *OM* upon his lips,
And leaves his body with the thought of Me,
Attains that end, O mighty Pṛthā's son.

My constant devotee, who keeps his mind 14
Intent on Me alone, comes soon to Me.
That great-souled one, once perfect, is not born 15
To live again in transience and pain.
Rebirth occurs in all the worlds but Mine; 16
Even in *Brahmā's* realm men are reborn;
For they who know the measurement of time 17
Know that a thousand *yugas** make one day
And that a thousand more are *Brahmā's* night.
Upon creation's dawn all things arise 18
From one potential store; and, as dusk falls,
Return to that, the great unmanifest.
This mass of beings, not by their own wills, 19
Passes through many births, and vanishes
Each time the night of *Brahmā* reappears;
And yet, beyond this universal store 20
Exists another Being, never lost
When all things are destroyed, which is Supreme. 21
There is My home, the highest state and goal,
From which no-one returns. True devotees 22
May reach that goal, in which all things reside,
And which pervades the whole created world.
Now I shall tell you of the time of death: 23
How when a *yogin* dies he's not reborn;
How other men return, O Bull of Bhāratas.
When gods of fire preside, in light of day, 24
Within the fortnight of the waxing Moon,
And in the half-year of the northern Sun,
Knowers of *Brahman* go to *Brahman* then.

When smoke and night prevail, with waning Moon, 25
Within the half-year of the southern Sun,
Who travels then attains the lunar light
And then returns. These paths of light and dark 26
That leave the world are so eternally;
One leads men back again, the other not.
No *yogins*, son of Pṛthā, are bemused 27
By knowledge of these paths, so follow them,
Always firm in *yoga* come what may.
Whatever great reward the *Vedas* yield 28
Whatever fruits by practices are won
Of sacrifice, austerity and gift,
These lesser gains the *yogins* all transcend
To reach My home, the one most ancient end."

Chapter 9

The Sovereign and Most Secret Wisdom

Then said the blessed Lord, "I shall reveal 1
To you, Arjuna, patient as you are,
How knowledge and its practice may unite;
From all misfortune this will make you free.
Of sciences it is the sovereign one, 2
Directly known, never thereafter lost,
The most profound, yet easy to perform,
Which purifies, whatever acts were done.
Those without faith in this eternal law 3
Come not to Me, O conqueror of foes,
But take the path of death and are reborn.
My form, unmanifest, pervades the world; 4
All creatures dwell in Me, not I in them.
Behold My power, which is their constant cause 5
And sustenance; for like a powerful wind, 6
Which moves in every region of the globe
Yet nowhere out of space, so all things rest
In Me alone. When one day of *Brahmā* 7
Draws to its close, in My own nature then,
O son of Kuntī, all things are dissolved.
At *Brahmā's* dawn I send them forth again,

In endless repetition moving them 8
By My own nature. Dhañanjaya, know 9
These actions do not bind Me, for I stay
Indifferent to them all and unattached.
By My mere presence nature generates 10
What moves, what does not move; from this one cause
The world revolves. Yet, in My human form, 11
I am ignored by fools, who do not know
My higher nature as the Lord of All.
Vain are their hopes, their works, what they believe; 12
Devoid of conscience, they are men possessed;
Demonic nature holds them in its thrall.
But those great souls whose nature is divine, 13
Adore Me only as the source of all,
Acknowledging I am immutable.
Full of praise and earnest in resolve, 14
They bow to Me, unswerving in their love.
Knowledge they give in sacrifice to Me, 15
Worshipping Me as One, or as the same
In different entities, or as the Lord
Whose visage reappears on every side.
I am the *Kratu** sacrifice itself; 16
I am the worship which the law enjoins;
I am the food the ancestors receive;
I am nutritious herbs of every kind;
I am the *mantra** chanted with the gift;
I am the butter clarified by fire;
I am the fire itself, the very act
Of offering; and, of this world, I am 17
The father, mother, grandsire, providence.

I alone am what is to be known,
The sound of *OM, Ṛg-Veda's** sacred verse,
And equally the *Sāma** and *Yajur**,
The final goal, dispenser of all fruits, 18
Lord, witness, home and refuge, friend to all,
The origin, foundation and the end,
The store of treasure, the undying seed.
Sunlight I give, and intermittent rain; 19
I am immortal life and also death;
I am existence and its opposite.
Those men who know the *Veda's* sacred rites, 20
Who drink the *soma** juice to purge their sins
And worship Me with *Vedic* sacrifice,
But pray for heaven, reach that holy world
Where Lord *Indra** presides, where they enjoy
The pleasures of the gods. They must return 21
From that immensity, their good deeds spent,
To re-emerge within the mortal world.
No *Vedic* ritual frees them from desire;
They quit this world, but merely to return.
But whoso thinks on Me as on himself, 22
With reverence for Me in everything,
As My disciple, he shall never want.
Those, full of faith, who worship other gods, 23
Worship Me also, but in ignorance;
For I alone enjoy all sacrifice; 24
I only am the sacrificial Lord.
Because they do not recognise Me thus,
They fail, O son of Kuntī, and return.

The devotees of gods go to the gods, 25
Of ancestors to them, and to the spirits
Spirits' devotees; so to Me, likewise,
My devotees return. Who offers Me 26
A flower, a piece of fruit, or water,
Or just a leaf, in token of his love,
His offer I accept, as from the pure.
Whatever you may do, whatever eat, 27
Whatever you may sacrifice, or give,
Whatever strict austerity you choose,
O son of Kuntī, offer that to Me.
By this the bonds of action shall be loosed, 28
And thus absolved from good and bad results,
Renouncing all, and free, come then to Me.
I am the same to all; by Me there are 29
None hated nor beloved. Who worships Me,
Devoted in his love, abides in Me,
And I in him. Even most wicked men, 30
Who worship only Me, deserve the name
Of righteousness, for they are well resolved;
Soon virtuous, they find eternal peace. 31
O Kuntī's son, proclaim this to the world,
That My disciple never can be lost,
Though born a woman or of lower caste; 32
For whoso looks for refuge in Myself
Attains to the Supreme. How much more then 33
The holy *brāhmins* and the saintly kings?
O Arjuna, you have attained this world,
A place of transience and sorrowful.

So worship Me, upon Me set your mind; 34
Give sacrifice to Me. Consider Me,
With constant heart, the highest aim of all.
Bow down to Me, become My devotee,
And you, indeed, shall come at last to Me."

Chapter 10
The Source of Divine Glory

"O mighty-armed Arjuna", said the Lord, 1
"Listen once more to My most sacred words,
In which you so delight. I utter them
For your well-being now. Not even hosts 2
Of gods and *ṛṣis** know My origin,
Since I Myself am their own single cause;
But he who knows Me as beginningless, 3
Unborn and only Lord of all the worlds,
That man is undeluded, freed from sin.
Intelligence and knowledge, truthfulness, 4
The power of judgment, patience and restraint,
Contentment, peace and equanimity,
Kindness and austerity of life,
Misery, pleasure, honour and disgrace,
Fear, courage, harmlessness, and birth and death: 5
All these conditions undergone by men
Arise indeed from Me; and from My mind, 6
Endowed with My own powers, came seven *ṛṣis*
And four progenitors* of all mankind.
All creatures in the world descend from them. 7
Whoever knows this glorious power of Mine

Partakes of it himself; and so wise men, 8
Who meditate on Me, bow down to Me
As that one source from which all things evolve.
Intent on Me, alive to nothing else, 9
They therefore speak of Me and teach themselves,
Living contentedly and in delight.
To these who love Me I convey this gift, 10
The power of reason leading them to Me;
And, out of My compassion, I destroy 11
With My strong lamp of wisdom their dark night;
In their loyal hearts I burn forever bright."

Arjuna then replied, "*Brahman* Supreme, 12
O source of purity, abode of all,
The *ṛṣis* and the godly Nārada, 13
Vyāsa, Devala and Asita*
Declare you Spirit, first before all gods,
Unborn, eternal, omnipresent Lord.
O Keśava, I know your words are true. 14
Though even gods and demons are misled
By how you may appear, you know your Self 15
By means of your own Self. O Lord Supreme,
O origin of all, O God of gods
And sovereign of the world, tell me in full 16
Of your divinity, how you exist,
Pervading by your attributes these worlds.
Tell me, O Lord, how I should think of you, 17
In what things I should contemplate you, Lord,
To come to know of you, unfailingly.

Tell of your *yoga* power, Janārdana, 18
And, with the sweet ambrosia of your speech,
Enumerate your splendours once again,
For I shall never hear your words in vain."

"O best of Kurus", said the Blessed Lord, 19
"My attributes are endless; I will speak
Of those which are divine and most pronounced.
O Prince Arjuna, conqueror of sleep, 20
I am the *Ātman* in the hearts of all;
Of beings the beginning, life and end.
I am Lord Viṣṇu* of the seven gods; 21
Amidst the stars I am resplendent Sun,
And Moon amongst the other heavenly orbs;
I am the flash of lightning in the storm.
I am the *Sāma* of the *Vedic* songs, 22
And I am Indra, Lord of all the gods.
I am the mind controlling every sense
And pure intelligence in all that lives.
I am Śaṃkara*, chief among the gods 23
Who drive away the evil of the world,
And Lord Kubera, deity of wealth.
Of elemental gods I am the fire;
Of mountains, I am Meru, holiest peak.
Know, also, son of Pṛthā, that I am 24
The highest priest, Bṛhaspati himself,
And mighty Skanda, champion of the gods.
I am the ocean, greatest of the seas,
And I am Bhṛgu, father of the wise. 25
Of words I am the single sound of *OM*;

Of offerings I am the sacrifice
In silent repetition in the mind;
And, of unmoving things, Himālaya;
Of trees, I am the holy Aśvattha; 26
And Nārada amongst the godly seers.
Of those who play the music of the gods
I am Citraratha; and Kapila
Of holy saints; and know Me as the horse
Uccaiśravas, who rose like nectar from 27
The churning sea; of elephants I am
Airayata, and, of all men, the king.
Of weapons I am Indra's thunderbolt; 28
I am the cow of plenty, Kāmadhuk;
I am the force of love, begetting all,
And, also, Vāsuki, the serpent king.
I am Ananta, greatest of snake-gods, 29
And Varunha, commander of the seas,
And Aryaman, chief forefather of men,
And mighty Yama*, measurer of life.
I am the king of demons, Prahlāda; 30
And I am time that calculates all change.
I am the regal lion amongst the beasts,
And Garuḍa of birds. Of things that purify 31
I am the wind; of those who wield the sword,
Lord Rāma*. Of fishes, I am the shark;
Of rivers I am Ganges; and in all 32
Creations the beginning, middle, end.
Of knowledge, I am knowledge of the Self;
Of disputants, I only seek the truth.

Of letters I am *a**; of compound words 33
I am the *dvandva** form; and I, indeed,
Am the eternity in passing time.
I give the fruits of action to the worlds;
And I am death, the universal thief, 34
And yet the source of all who are to live.
Of what is feminine, I am the gifts
Of fame and beauty, constancy and speech,
Of memory, patience and intelligence.
I am the finest of all songs of praise; 35
Of poetic metres, I am Gāyatṛ.
Of months I am the Mārgaśirṣa month;
Of seasons I am Spring, the time of flowers.
I am the gambler's winning cast of dice; 36
I am the fire of energetic men;
The victory, as well as the endeavour;
I am, indeed, the goodness in the good.
I am Dhanañjaya of Pāṇḍavas, 37
And Vāsudeva of the Vṛṣṇī tribe.
I am Vyāsa of the ancient seers
And sage Uśanas, foremost of the wise;
I am the sceptre of avenging kings 38
And equity amongst aggressive states.
I am the silence of all secret things,
Knowledge of those who know, and seed of all. 39
What moves, what does not move, cannot exist
Without Myself. O scorcher of all foes, 40
My godly splendour is without an end:
These are but glimpses of My attributes.

Wherever there is greatness, brilliance, strength, 41
That is but one effect of My true light.
Yet what is this diversity to you? 42
Know only that My merest part maintains
This world entire and all that it contains."

Chapter 11
The Vision of the Universal Form

"By your compassionate words, "Arjuna said, 1
"Which teach what is the Self and what is not,
My own delusion has been quite dispelled.
How things begin and end, how you remain, 2
O, Lotus-eyed, immutable and great:
From you, profoundly, I have heard all this.
And yet, O Lord Supreme, I still desire 3
To see your form as sovereign lord of all.
If, in your judgement, I am not too weak, 4
Then show me this, the vision that I seek."

The Blessed Lord replied to Pṛthā's son: 5
"See then My forms divine of every hue,
Thousand on thousand. See the gods themselves, 6
The twelve *Ādityas* of the heavenly sphere,
The bright *Vasus*, *Rudras* and twin *Aśvins**,
The roaring *Maruts*, deities of wind,
Unnumbered marvels never seen before.
Behold, O Bhārata, My body here, 7
In which the mighty universe is set,
Both moving and unmoving parts of it.
Behold what you desire, O valiant one!

I give you eyes divine to see this sight, 8
For mortal eyes are blind to *yoga's* might."

To Pṛthā's son the Great Lord then revealed 9
His universal shape, as *Īśvara**.
The scents of heaven garlanded that form 10 - 11
And robes resplendent shone on every side.
With countless faces full of eyes and mouths,
And heavenly weapons lifted up on high,
Each limb adorned with lovely ornaments,
He ruled unbounded, marvellous to behold.
That mighty Being shone with glorious light - 12
A thousand Suns at once in heaven blazing -
And, held within the God of gods own form, 13
The son of Pāṇḍu saw the very world,
The universe, divided manifold,
Yet resting there, as one, within the Lord.

His hair on end with rapture at this scene, 14
With joined palms and lowering his head,
Possessed with wonder, Dhanañjaya spoke:
"In your own body, Lord, I see the gods, 15
And hosts of creatures, every kind of thing:
The Lord *Brahmā* upon his lotus seat,
The seers of old and serpents of the skies.
I see you, Lord, so infinite in form; 16
On every side I see your myriad arms,
Your bellies, mouths and eyes; there is no end,
No place where you begin, nor one between.
O Lord of every form, O Lord Supreme,

Adorned with crowns, with club and discus armed, 17
A radiant mass of universal light,
Of blazing fire and bright effulgent Suns,
My eyes can barely see your boundless might.
O Lord Supreme, O Lord, immutable, 18
You who alone are worthy to be known,
Safe refuge of the world, and guardian Prince
Of that eternal Law that governs all,
You are, I deem, the ancient Soul of Man.
As I behold you, infinite in power, 19
Alpha and Omega of all that is,
With Sun and Moon for eyes and mighty arms
Commanding every side, I see your face
Blazing with purest fire, to warm the world
With your benevolence. From heaven to earth 20
You fill each mote of air and part of space.
The three worlds tremble at your awful form.
These gods, incarnate here as men of war, 21
Enter your mighty frame in fearful prayer,
Praising with joined palms; whilst crowds of seers,
And men of godly power, entreat you for
The welfare of the world, singing your praise
With sweet resounding hymns. The gods of fire 22
And storm, free spirits of the air and great
Musicians of the celestial spheres,
The shining being in the eternal Sun
And powerful gods whom men propitiate,
Ancestors of the race and great perfected men:
All these, astounded, gaze upon your form.

Seeing you thus, O Lord of mighty-arms, 23
Huge beyond measure, very worlds themselves
Are filled with terror of your eyes and limbs,
Your thighs and stomachs, mouths replete with tusks;
And I myself am frightened deep within 24
To see you blaze with colour to the sky,
With yawning mouths and vasty burning eyes.
My courage fails and, with it, all repose.
How can I know the quarters of the globe, 25
When in your tusky mouths I see those fires
Which herald now the dusk and end of time?
I have no peace; I pray be merciful,
O Lord of gods, and only home of all.
Into your fearsome mouths these ranks of kings, 26 - 27
Protectors of the earth, rush without pause,
Great Dhṛtarāṣṭra's breed and all the rest,
Proud Bhīṣma, Droṇa, Karṇa's worthy son,
And even those of our Pāṇḍava host.
Between your teeth they stick, heads ground to dust.
As river torrents hasten to the sea, 28 - 29
As moths fly fast to die in blazing fires,
So do these heroes in the world of men
In your dread mouth annihilate themselves.
Your tongues cast down the worlds on every side 30
Into the fiery chasm of your throat.
The universe itself, O Viṣṇu, burns
From those fierce rays that emanate from you.
I bow to Thee for mercy, Lord Supreme. 31
Who are you, Lord? What is this awful form?

For though I cannot know what you intend,
To know you in yourself is my true end."

To Arjuna the Blessed Lord replied: 32
"I am that Time which overturns the world;
Which, even now, destroys all creatures here.
Were you, Arjuna, to ignore your part,
Yet would they perish still who stand arrayed
In hostile arms. Yet rise and conquer them; 33
Enjoy your fame, and win unrivalled
Lordship in this world. Already are they slain,
For I myself have killed these warriors.
Be but an instrument, O mighty man,
Who holds the well-stringed bow in either hand.
Drona and Bhīṣma, Jayadratha too, 34
The mighty Karṇa, fathered by the Sun,
All these, and others unsurpassed in arms,
Are killed by Me, but you kill them no less.
Fight now and conquer, kill without distress."

Trembling at Kṛṣṇa's speech, with joined palms, 35
His crowned head lowered to his Master's feet,
Arjuna then replied, with stammered words:
"O joyous Lord, the world resounds in praise, 36
Whilst demons fly in turmoil at your wrath,
And hosts of saints in reverence bow down.
What else, O mighty One, greatest of all, 37
Cause of *Brahmā* himself? O Infinite,
O Lord of all the gods, abode of this

Whole universe, O never-ending God,
Being and non-being, beyond them both,
First cause of all, and now, since time began, 38
The ancient Spirit of embodied life,
The final refuge and the goal of all,
Knower and knowable - your endless forms
Pervade this universe. You are the gods 39
Of waters, winds and fire, of death, of Moon,
Prajāpati, the guardian of life.
All hail to you! Great Father, hail, hail, hail!
A thousand salutations, hail to you!
In front, behind, on every side, all hail, 40
O Absolute, O infinite in power,
O Lord of valour, immanent in all.
Whatever I have said without due care, 41 - 42
With gross presumption or familiar love,
Addressing you as Kṛṣṇa, or my friend,
Or by your family name, as if you were
My comrade on the field, in disregard
Of your own greatness; and what disrespect
You have endured, whatever levity,
Whilst walking, resting, seated, at repast,
Or when we were with others or alone,
Forgive all this, I beg, O boundless Lord.
O you who are the Father of the world 43
With all its moving and unmoving realms,
O you are what this world, in truth, adores.
O Lord, of majesty beyond compare,
Whence comes another greater than yourself,
Even within the order of three worlds?

I bow before you, prostrate at your feet. 44
Be gracious, dearest Lord, forgive my faults,
As father to his son, as friend to friend,
Or as devoted lover to his love.
At seeing what no mortal eye has seen, 45
I am replete with joy, and yet my mind
Is paralysed by fear. Have mercy, Lord,
The home of all repose, show me your form
Crowned as before, possessed of four strong arms, 46
With mace and disc in hand. O fearful God,
Whose body is the universe entire,
Be but that Kṛṣṇa whom I most desire."

"By grace, Arjuna," said the blessed Lord, 47
"To you alone this vision was revealed,
My incandescent, universal form,
Unborn and boundless, never seen by Man.
My power of *yoga* brought this to your eyes.
No *Vedic* study, sacrifice, nor gift, 48
No ritual, nor severe austerity
Can summon up this sight for any man
Besides yourself, O mighty warrior,
Born of Kuru race. Be not bewildered, 49
Nor stunned by fright at this dread shape of Mine.
Fearless, with joy, see Me as man again."

With these consoling words, that mighty Lord, 50
Who was, in truth, the Spirit of the world,
Appeared once more in Kṛṣṇa's comely form.

"Lord, who sustains us all", Arjuna said, 51
Your gentle form makes every terror cease;
My nature is restored, my mind at peace."

Then spoke the Blessed Lord: "The gods themselves 52
Have long desired to see that rarest form,
Vouchsafed to you. What you have seen of Me 53
No offering can win, nor sacrifice,
Austerity, nor gift, nor *Vedic* rites.
By simple love alone I may be known, 54
And seen, Arjuna, in reality;
For by such love, O scorcher of all foes,
You enter into Me. For he who works 55
Devoted to Myself, who makes of Me
His one and final end, who loves Me only
Free from worldly ties, who bears no hatred
For a living thing: one such as he,
O valiant son of Pāṇḍu, comes to Me."

Chapter 12
The Way of Love

"Which are the better versed," Arjuna asked, 1
"In *yoga's* practice: those who worship you,
Or those who worship the unmanifest,
The one, unchanging *Brahman*? What is best?"

"The better *yogins*", said the Blessed Lord, 2
"Are those who ever contemplate Myself,
With steadfast mind, unshakeable in faith.
For those, indeed, who contemplate *Brahman*, 3
Beyond all definition and all thought,
The indestructible, unmanifest,
The One, immovable, outside of time,
Such men of even mind, with sense restrained, 4
Intent on the prosperity of all,
They reach Me also; yet their goal is hard. 5
For all embodied creatures such a way
Is greater trouble than to worship Me.
For those who offer all their acts to Me, 6
Regard Me as supreme and meditate
On Me alone, eschewing every thought,
They truly worship Me. For such as these,
Who set their minds on union with Me,

O son of Pṛthā, I become ere long 7
Their saviour from the ocean of despair,
The fitful round of endless birth and death.
Attend to Me, Arjuna, firm in heart, 8
And so ensure your dwelling place in Me
Beyond this mortal life; or failing this, 9
O Dhanañjaya, train your wilful mind,
And strive, by constant practice, for that end.
If this exceeds your strength, then let your acts 10
Be done for My sake; for by this alone
Perfection may be finally achieved;
Or even, merely, cast aside the fruits, 11
Seeking repose in Me, with self-control.
Just as the act of repetitious thought 12
Is far surpassed by knowledge, so indeed
Is meditation more esteemed than that.
Yet, for a man incapable of these,
Renunciation is the proper way,
For peace attends the sacrifice of gain.
He who befriends all creatures, hating none, 13
Compassionate, without the thought of 'mine',
Devoid of ego, patient and content,
Unmoved by pain and pleasure, self-controlled, 14
Steady in contemplation, sure of mind,
His thought and reason steadfastly on Me:
Who loves Me thus is specially dear to Me.
He who does not agitate the world, 15
Nor whom the world disturbs, unmoved by fear,
Beyond impatience, pleasure or regret:
Such a one is specially dear to Me.

He who depends on nothing, pure at heart, 16
Who does not hesitate when called to act,
Without anxiety or desire to please,
Whose undertakings offer no reward:
Such a one is specially dear to Me.
He who does not boast at each success, 17
Nor frets at failure, grieves at any loss,
Covets no thing, renounces good and bad,
Who, come what may, remains devoted still:
Such a one is specially dear to Me.
He who is the same to friend and foe, 18
In honour and dishonour, heat and cold,
Unmoved in pleasure or in misery,
Free from attachment to the world of sense,
Equal in the face of praise and blame, 19
Imbued with silence, ever satisfied,
With no home but Myself: one such as this,
Steadfast and full of love, is dear to Me.
Who follows *dharma*, this immortal law,
Who, full of faith, devotes himself to Me,
Whoever thus regards Me as Supreme,
Is held most dear, highest in My esteem."

Chapter 13
Spirit and Nature

"What are nature, Spirit, body and the Soul? 1
What is knowledge? What does one need to know?
I wish to learn of these," Arjuna said.
"O Keśava, O Lord, come to my aid."

"This body, where the fruit of deeds are reaped,
Is called the field", replied the Blessed Lord.
"Men call the knower of the field the Soul;
You indeed should know that I Myself 2
Am truly knower of the field in all.
To separate the knower from the field
Is really knowledge; and that field itself, 3
Its properties and how they fluctuate,
What causes lead to what diverse effects,
Who really is the knower of the field
And what his powers are: all this, in brief,
I will reveal. Of these in sacred hymns 4
The seers have sung, in words that treat of *Brahman*,
Full of reason, certain and distinct.
The field is this: the five great elements*, 5
Ego, intellect and perceptual powers
And forces that enable men to act,
Such as by tongue or hand, discursive mind,
The senses' fivefold objects and, indeed,

All unseen nature; desire and hatred, 6
Pleasure, pain, intelligence and will:
These constitute the field and all its forms.
Humility and lack of all pretence, 7
Non-injury to any living thing,
Forbearance, honesty, and serving those
Who teach the way of truth; the purity
Of body and of mind, firmness of will,
And self-control in face of every test,
Withdrawal from the objects of each sense, 8
Absence of ego, and reflecting on
The miseries of old age, birth and death,
Of sickness and of pain; avoiding bonds, 9
Especially those of home and wife and son,
Indifference to whatever may occur,
Unswerving love for Me as for oneself, 10
Resort to places far from humankind,
Distaste for impure company of men,
The constant study of the Self within, 11
And understanding of the final end:
All these are means to knowledge of the Self.
What is opposed to that is ignorance.
And now I shall relate what should be known, 12
Which, once acknowledged, gives eternal life.
That *Brahman*, the Supreme, does not begin;
Nor is It said to be, nor not to be;
But It envelops all, with hands and feet, 13
With eyes and heads and mouths in every place,
With ears that hear throughout the universe, 14
Possessing none, but shining through them all,
Quite unattached and yet supporting all,
Devoid of qualities, outside all things - 15
The moving and unmoved - and yet within,
Too fine to be perceived, far off yet near,

As though divided into many parts, 16
Yet undivided and sustaining all,
Which It creates and likewise It devours.
It is, they say, the light of every light, 17
Beyond all darkness. It is the knowledge.
Dwelling in all hearts, the goal of knowing,
And the knowable. Thus have I told you 18
Of the known field, of knowledge, and of that
Which should be known. Thus taught, My devotees
Are fitted then for union with Me.
Spirit and nature are beginningless; 19
And from eternal nature rise *guṇas*
And every form of body, mind and sense;
Whilst as aware of pleasure and of pain, 20
The Spirit may be called the cause of both.
Seated in nature, Spirit then perceives 21
The *guṇas* sprung from it; attached to these,
He is reborn in good or evil wombs.
As witness, He permits and nourishes, 22
The sole enjoyer of the changing field.
Hence is that Spirit called, embodied thus,
The Mighty Lord, the Highest Self of all.
That man who knows the Spirit in this way 23
And nature, with its threefold qualities,
He is not born again, whatever acts
He may indeed perform. Some see the Self 24
By meditation on the Self within;
Some find Him by the power of intellect;
Others by acts in service of the Lord.
Some, also, worship, ignorant of these, 25
As they have heard from others. Even they,
Remembering what they hear, pass over death.

O scion of the house of Bharata, 26
Things that are born, the moving or the still,
Are only the apparent union
Of field and knower; but he truly sees 27
Who sees the Lord in all, deathless in death.
And once the Lord is everywhere descried, 28
The Self, by self, can never then be harmed,
For who sees thus attains the highest goal.
Who knows that nature undertakes all acts, 29
Knows, therefore, that the Self is actionless,
And when he sees all separate things as One, 30
In evolution from that One alone,
Becomes *Brahman* Itself, O Kuntī's son.
For this, the Highest Self, does not begin; 31
Beyond the *guṇas*, and immovable,
It lives in body, free from every act,
Untouched by action; just as purest space, 32
Pervading all by fineness, is not marred.
For Self, in every body, has no taint.
Just as the Sun illumines all this earth, 33
So does embodied Self shine on this field,
The whole created world, O Bhārata.
That man, whose eye of knowledge separates, 34
As quite distinct, the knower and the field,
And frees himself from belief in nature's form,
Possessed of wisdom, goes to the Supreme."

Chapter 14
The Three Guṇas

The Blessed Lord then said: "I shall declare 1
This knowledge, which exceeds all, once again,
For, learning this indeed, the sage attains
To liberation from all earthly bonds,
And all who make this knowledge their resort 2
Find unity in Me. They are not born
Within this universe, nor when it is
Dissolved are they disturbed. O Bhārata,
My own great nature is the womb of all, 3
In which I place the seed, intelligence.
Whatever's born, from whatsoever source, 4
My nature is its womb, the seed is Mine,
And I the Father. Produced by nature, 5
Three *guṇas* of *sattva*, *rajas*, *tamas*
Bind the Soul, which lives within the body
Undestroyed. *Sattva*, O son of Kuntī, 6
Though free from evil, stainless, full of light,
Yet by attachment fastens on the Soul
The thoughts of "I am happy" and "I know".
Hear now, O sinless one, how *rajas* works: 7
Its passion colours the embodied Soul,

And is the source of thirst for fruits of acts
And strong attachment to the act itself;
Whilst *tamas*, born of ignorance, deludes, 8
With heedlessness, with indolence and sleep.
In *sattva*, then, the Soul wants happiness, 9
In *rajas* action, and in *tamas*, sloth,
Enshrouding knowledge and neglecting care.
If two *guṇas* succumb before the third, 10
That one predominates in its effect.
O Lord of Bharatas, when *sattva* rules 11
The light of knowledge fills the gates of sense;
But when activity, desire and haste, 12
Unrest and greed arise, *rajas* prevails;
Whilst *tamas* brings the absence of all light, 13
Hence negligence, inertia and mistake.
If death confronts the Soul when *sattva* rules, 14
It reaches then that heaven, devoid of sin,
Where dwell the worshippers of highest gods;
If at a time of *rajas*, it is born 15
Among those bound to action; whilst that one
Who dies in *tamas* finds a brutish womb.
Good actions yield fruits *sāttvika* and pure; 16
Actions in *rajas* culminate in pain;
Whilst those in *tamas* foster ignorance.
Sattva gives knowledge, *rajas* avarice, 17
From *tamas* there emerges carelessness,
Delusion and, in fine, stupidity.
Those who live in *sattva* rise to gods; 18
Dwellers in *rajas* stay in human form;
Those in *tamas* degenerate to beasts.

The sage who sees that only *guṇas* act, 19
And knows what is beyond, transcends them all,
Although they are his body's very cause; 20
And, freed from birth, from death, old age and strife,
He reaches Me and finds immortal life."

At this, Arjuna asked, "How is he known? 21
How does he go beyond? How does he live?
O Lord, on this what guidance can you give?"

"O Pāṇḍava", the Blessed Lord replied, 22
"He who does not hate whatever comes,
The light of *sattva*, action of *rajas*,
Or that delusion which *tamas* creates,
Nor longs for any one when it has gone,
Who sits unmoved, whom *guṇas* cannot shake, 23
Who knows they act, but rests within Himself,
Who is the same in pleasure and in pain 24
And looks alike on earth and stone and gold,
To whom the loved and unloved are as one,,
Who stays content in honour and disgrace,
Untouched by praise or blame, to friend or foe 25
Impartially the same, who has renounced
All deeds and their effects - the sages say
Of such a one that he has crossed beyond.
He who serves Me with never-failing love, 26
Who thus has passed beyond the *guṇas'* power,
For union with *Brahman* is prepared.
For that immortal *Brahman* rests in Me, 27
Lawful, in constant bliss, eternally."

Chapter 15
The Supreme Spirit

Then said the Blessed Lord, "This world below 1
Is like the holy fig tree, Aśvattha*,
Which men believe has everlasting life.
Rooted in *Brahman's* nature high above,
It branches downwards, leaved in *Vedic* verse.
Whoever knows this universal tree,
He knows the *Veda*, knows the root of all.
On every side its branches spread afar, 2
Nourished by *guṇas*, sprouting buds of sense,
Whilst underneath its roots proliferate
And bind with acts the world of humankind;
But men do not perceive it in this way, 3
How it began, how it exists or ends.
When that strong sword, detachment, has cut down
The Aśvattha*, and severed its deep roots,
That goal is to be found whence none return. 4
Who seeks this end decides, 'I will resort
To that primeval Self from which life flows.'
The evil of attachment overcome, 5
And ever dwelling there within the Self,
Devoid of pride, released from all desire,
Freed from the poles of pleasure and of pain,
Such men, no more deluded, reach that goal.

No Sun illumines it, nor Moon, nor fire, 6
For that is My Abode, from which no man
Who reaches it shall ever thence return.
A spark, or ray, of My eternal Self, 7
Becomes a living Soul within the world
And, in a body, draws around Himself
The fivefold senses and discursive mind,
Which He takes with Him when He comes and goes, 8
As scent of flowers is borne upon the wind.
This is the Lord who governs eye and ear, 9
Organs of touch, of taste, of smell, and mind,
The one enjoyer of what sense conveys.
Deluded men are unaware of Him, 10
Of when He comes and goes with birth and death,
Or when, amidst the *guṇas*, He remains.
They only see who see with wisdom's eye,
Intent on *yoga*, finding Him within; 11
Not those, devoid of intellect, who strive
With minds untrained by true austerity.
Know this, Arjuna - that the light is Mine 12
Which shines within the Sun upon this world,
Illuminates the Moon and every fire.
I penetrate the earth, supporting all 13
With My vitality; as sapid Moon
I nourish every herb. Within the body 14
Of each living thing, I am the fire
Which, joined with breaths, consumes the fourfold food;
And I reside within the hearts of all, 15
Dispensing knowledge, memory and their loss.

Who reads the *Vedas* there discovers Me;
The words of the *Vedānta* are My words,
And he who knows them is My very Self.
Two kinds of beings constitute this world: 16
Creatures that perish and their inmost seed,
Which - it is said - is quite immutable;
And yet, distinct from these, the Highest Self 17
And never changing Lord of triple worlds,
Whom wise men call Supreme, pervades them all,
And nourishes their life. Transcending then 18
What perishes or not, above them all,
Within the *Veda* and within the world,
I am entitled *Puruṣottama*.
Whoever, undeluded, knows Me thus 19
As Highest Spirit, thereby knows all things,
And with his very being worships Me,
O scion of the house of Bharata.
To you, O Arjuna, I offer this, 20
The hidden teaching of the Holy Way*;
By knowing which one wins, O sinless one,
The prize of wisdom, with all duty done."

Chapter 16

Divine and Demonic Qualities

Then said the Blessed Lord to Arjuna: 1
"Lack of all fear, and purity of mind,
A firm resolve to follow *yoga's* path,
Giving of alms, and worship, self-control,
The study of the scriptures, honesty,
Austerity and absence of all harm, 2
A love of truth, renouncing of desire,
Freedom from anger and all calumny,
Serenity, compassion for the creatures
Of the world, restraint in sense perception,
No useless movement of the tongue or limbs,
Gentleness and modesty to all,
Boldness in action, patience, fortitude, 3
Cleanliness of body and of mind,
The absence of all hatred and of pride:
These are the marks, O son of Bharata,
Of men, whose nature is, by birth, divine.
Whilst arrogance, hypocrisy, conceit, 4
Coarse language, anger, ignorance of truth,
Are signs, O Pārtha, of demonic birth.
The godly state engenders one result: 5
The liberation of those men so born;

Whilst those are bound who are demoniac.
Grieve not, O Pāṇḍava, for you were born
As one of godly nature. The world contains 6
Two types of beings, demon and divine.
The godly ones I have described at length;
Now hear Me speak, O Pārtha, of the rest.
What actions serve the proper ends of Man 7
Demonic men ignore; nor do they see
What actions to avoid; nor have they truth,
Nor purity, nor well-conducted lives.
Such men proclaim, 'There is no truth, no Lord, 8
No moral law for this whole universe -
Conceived in lust, born of desire, what else?'
Possessed by this, these souls despoiled of hope, 9
Of narrow intellect and fearsome deeds,
Rise up as the destroyers of the world.
Insatiable desire, pretence and pride 10
Inform their minds; deceived by false ideas,
Their acts are tainted thus with impure will.
Sensual enjoyment is their highest end; 11
'Beyond that - nothing' is their firm belief,
Till death alone removes their countless cares.
Abandoning themselves to lust and wrath, 12
And tethered by innumerable false hopes,
They struggle to obtain by unjust means
The wealth to spend on pleasures of the flesh.
'This thing I seized today; this new desire 13
I shall indulge; this thing is mine, and soon
These riches shall be mine as well. By me

That enemy was slain; by my hand also 14
Will these others die. For I am lord,
Enjoyer of the world and its success,
A powerful and a pleasure-loving man,
Well born and rich. Who else can rival me? 15
I sacrifice, and I will offer gifts;
I will rejoice.' And so deluded thus,
Bewildered by imaginary thoughts, 16
Enmeshed in dreams, addicted to their lust,
Such men degenerate, until they fall
Into the mouths of hell. These pompous men,
Stubborn, and enamoured of their wealth, 17
Make play of sacrifice, and disregard
What scriptural authority ordains.
Selfish and proud, lustful, obsessed with power, 18
They burn with anger, hating Me within
And where in other bodies I am found.
Repeatedly I cast these evil men 19
Within the wombs of cruel, rapacious beasts.
O Son of Kuntī, these deluded ones, 20
Born from demonic wombs from life to life,
Pass into states more dreadful than before
And, so degraded, never come to Me.
Three ways converge upon the gates of hell: 21
Lust, wrath and greed, destructive of the self.
O Son of Kuntī, quite forsake them all.
That man who does not pass these gates of doom 22
Cares for himself and reaches the Supreme,

But he who shuns the scriptures' sacred law 23
And acts upon the impulse of desire,
His life is unfulfilled; he finds no joy,
Nor comes to the Supreme. Make then that law 24
The measure of your choice, to act or not,
And so, upon this field, do what you ought,
Aware of what the ancient law has taught."

Chapter 17
The Three Forms of Faith

"What is the place of those who sacrifice, 1
Who are endued with faith", Arjuna asked,
"Yet ignorant of what the scriptures state?
What *guṇas*, then, O Lord, predominate?"

The Blessed Lord replied, "The faith of those 2
Embodied on this earth is of three forms -
The *sāttvic* faith, *rājasic* and *tāmasic* -
Which follow from the nature of each man.
Hear now of these. To his own nature each 3
Man's faith conforms, for man is made of faith;
As is his faith, so is he in himself.
Those men of *sattva* worship only gods,
But many kinds of demons are invoked
By the *rājasic*, whilst those of *tamas*
Call on the very spirits of the dead.
Those who torment themselves with violent pain 5
In opposition to the scriptural law,
Who are possessed by lust and self-conceit,
Who torture their own bodies senselessly, 6
In ignorance that I am dwelling there,
Are devotees of these demonic powers.

Of three kinds, also, is the food men like, 7
As are their types of worship and of gift,
And their austerities. Hear now of this:
Foods rich in oil, which offer life and strength, 8
Promoting health and lasting energy,
Which cheer the heart and satisfy the taste,
By men of *sāttvic* nature are preferred.
The foods that are acidic, bitter, salt, 9
The over-hot, the pungent, burning, dry,
Which lead to pain, grief, sickness and disease,
These foods are what *rājasic* men prefer;
Whilst stale and tasteless, putrid, stinking food, 10
Leavings of others, food stored over-long,
What is impure, *tāmasic* men desire.
That worship which the sacred law prescribes, 11
Offered by men who look for no reward,
With mind intent on nothing else at all,
That worship only is the *sāttvic* form;
But that which seeks some fruit, or to impress, 12
Know that to be, O best of Bhāratas,
No more than worship in *rājasic* form.
Unlawful worship, offering no food, 13
Devoid of gifts and with defective song,
Empty of faith, is governed by *tamas*.
Due reverence for gods, for those born twice, 14
For teachers and the wise, an honest life,
Both pure and continent, and harm to none:
These are the body's whole austerity.
That speech which does not vex, but pleases all, 15
Speech which is true, conferring benefit,

And recitation of the sacred texts,
All these are called austerity of speech.
Serenity and silence, kindliness, 16
And self-control and no duplicity,
These constitute austerity of mind.
This triple rule of body, speech and mind, 17
Practised with faith by dedicated men
Who want no fruits, the wise call *sāttvica*.
But if austerity is practised here 18
To win some favour, honour or respect,
And done with ostentation, then indeed,
It is *rājasic*, transitory and brief.
If practised, by some whim, to hurt oneself, 19
Or with intent to ruin someone else,
It is *tāmasic*; so the wise declare.
That gift most properly due in time and place, 20
Offered to one most worthy to receive,
Without regard to any recompense,
Is held to be a truly *sāttvic* gift;
But if one gives expecting some return, 21
Or benefit, or gives reluctantly,
That gift is called *rājasic*. One given 22
At an inauspicious time, or unfit place,
To undeserving men, or carelessly,
Or even with contempt, is *tāmasic*.
The words of *OM, Tat, Sat** are said to be 23
The triple designation of *Brahman*;
By these emerged the class of *Brāhmaṇas*,
The *Vedic* scriptures and all sacrifice;

And thus with *OM* the proper acts begin 24
Of sacrifice, austerity and gift,
For those who follow the *Vedāntic* law.
Likewise they are performed with *Tat* by those
Who search for freedom, unconcerned with fruits;
Whilst *Sat*, O Pārtha, means reality, 26
And, also, goodness and auspicious acts.
Complete devotion is considered *Sat*,
In sacrifice, austerity and gift 27
And actions done entirely for the Lord;
But that performed, O Pārtha, without faith, 28
Though sacrifice, austerity or gift,
Is called *Asat*, for, as the wise have taught,
In this world and the next, it comes to naught."

Chapter 18
Liberation

Arjuna asked, "O Lord of mighty arms, 1
You have described two ways men may renounce.
Are they the same, O slayer of Keśi?
I wish to know what difference this may be."

The Blessed Lord replied to Arjuna: 2
"One way, the wise declare, is to renounce
All acts which have the motive of desire,
The other, to abandon all the fruits.
Some say 'all acts are bad - relinquish them!', 3
Whilst others say that works of sacrifice,
Austerity and gift should be exempt.
Hear from Me now, O best of Bhāratas, 4
The final resolution of this point.
Sacrifice, austerity and gift 5
Should be performed, O tiger amongst men.
They help, indeed, to purify the wise,
But even these, O Pārtha, should be done 6
Without attachment or desire for fruits;
Such is My best and resolute belief.
Renunciation has, in truth, three forms.

Because neglect of duty is a wrong, 7
Renouncing, in delusion, such an act
Has been declared *tāmasic* by the wise.
He, also, who avoids an act from fear, 8
Renounces merely in *rājasic* form,
Finding no freedom in such abstinence;
But when, Arjuna, something must be done 9
And duty only motivates the act,
So that the actor has no thought of gain,
Renunciation, then, is deemed *sāttvic*.
For he who has renounced in such a way, 10
With keen intelligence and free from doubt,
Imbued with *sattva*, does not hate those acts
Which are discomforting; nor does he cling
To those which men enjoy. In truth, no man 11
Who thinks he is embodied can renounce
His every act. To give up fruits of action
Is enough to earn the name renouncer.
The three results of evil, good, or both 12
Of these conjoined, come after death to all,
Excepting those who truly have renounced.
O mighty-armed Arjuna, learn from Me 13
What five-fold causes lead to every act,
According to that wisdom which prescribes
How action ends with knowledge of the Self.
The body as the seat of every state, 14
The agent, or enjoyer, of the act,
Organs of sense and functions they perform,
And, lastly, a presiding deity:

All these, whatever act one undertakes, 15
By body, mind or speech, for good or ill,
Cause that same act; and so, whoever thinks,
Without intelligence, of his own Self 16
As agent, fails, through feeble-mindedness,
To see in action how things come to pass;
But he who has no thought of selfishness, 17
Who, even whilst he kills, remains untouched,
In truth he is not bound, nor does he kill.
For every act the impulse is the same, 18
Consisting of the knowledge and the known,
And then the knower, these three all combined;
Whilst in the act a unity is made
Of instrument, the agent and the end.
The science of the *guṇas* teaches how 19
All knowledge falls into distinctive types
And, likewise, action and the agent, too.
Listen now to what I have to say:
Knowledge by which one sees the Self in all, 20
As substance that can never be destroyed,
Inseparate in separated things,
That, you can be sure, is *sāttvica*;
But that by which one sees a separate self, 21
Distinct from others, in each various thing,
Is called *rājasica*; whilst that which clings, 22
Devoid of reason, to just one effect,
As if it were the one reality,
Though quite untrue and trivial in itself,
That is declared to be *tāmasica*.

An ordered action, free from love or hate, 23
Without attachment or desire for fruits,
Is *sāttvica*; but acts performed for pleasure 24
Or self-pride, or done with undue effort,
Are described as acts *rājaṣica*;
And those begun regardless of all loss, 25
Or injury or other consequence,
And unaware of what can be performed,
They are deluded acts, *tāmasica*.
A *sāttvic* agent does not claim success, 26
Nor lack of it; his actions have no taint
Of selfishness. He acts with fortitude,
With vigour, though detached; whilst those impure, 27
Or cruel, or passionate, are deemed *rajasic*.
They covet fruits of action, full of greed,
Moved by elation, downcast by their grief.
Vulgarity and pride, despondency, 28
Unsteadiness, deceit and wickedness,
Procrastination, indolence - by these
The agent under *tamas* is beset.
Listen, O Dhanañjaya, whilst I say 29
How intellect and fortitude themselves
Take triple forms, caused by the *guṇas'* power.
That intellect which knows of work and rest, 30
Of rightful actions and their opposites,
Which sees the cause of fear and fearlessness,
Of bondage and the goal of liberty,
That intellect is *sāttvic*, O Pārtha.
Whenever law is wrongly understood 31
And what is to be done is ill perceived,

That is *rājasic* intellect, O Prince.
If lawlessness usurps the name of law,
And all is seen entirely in reverse, 32
Then *tamas* is the ruling quality.
When thought and breath and senses are restrained 33
By fortitude derived from *yoga's* power,
That constant strength is *sāttvic*, O Pārtha;
But when restraint is driven by desire 34
For what right action, wealth and pleasure bring,
That is, indeed, *rājasic* fortitude;
Whilst that by which a fool does not give up 35
His sleep, fear, sorrow, misery and lust,
That is *tāmasic* fortitude, O Prince.
Now hear Me tell of threefold happiness, 36
So that you may, O Lord of Bhāratas,
Learn true delight and reach the end of pain.
That happiness, like poison at first taste, 37
Like nectar in the end, conceived in light
From knowledge of the Self, is called *sāttvic*;
But that which comes from contact by a sense, 38
Like nectar first, like poison finally,
That is the *rajas* form of happiness.
That happiness which all along remains 39
Deluded and oblivious of Self,
And caused by error, idleness and sleep,
That happiness is called *tāmasika*.
Nothing on earth, nor with the gods above, 40
Avoids three *guṇas*, born from nature's womb.
Thus do the fourfold classes find the paths 41
Of wisdom, war, of trading and of work,

By distribution of the *guṇas'* powers,
Which thus determine each man's qualities.
The duties of a *Brāhmaṇa* are these: 42
To be serene, endued with self-restraint,
Austere and pure of mind, patient, sincere,
Possessed of knowledge and the power to judge,
Imbued with faith in what the scriptures teach:
Such are the duties which his nature yields.
Valour and boldness, fortitude and skill, 43
Unwillingness to quit the field of war,
The rightful exercise of sovereign power
And generosity to one and all:
To these the *Kṣatriya* devotes his life.
The nature of the *Vaiśya* is to trade, 44
To plough the fields, to care for herds and flocks;
Whilst *Śūdras* are, by nature, born to serve.
Devoted to their duty, men may come 45
To reach perfection which surpasses all.
Hear, then, Arjuna, how this may be done.
Those men, who through their duty worship Him 46
Who is progenitor of all that lives,
And who pervades the world, attain that end.
For one's own duty, even without worth, 47
Is better far than others' well performed.
Who does that duty which his birth entails
Commits no sin, for though admixed with harm
It should be done. All things that men perform 48
Are wrapped in evil, just as fire in smoke.
Those men whose intellect is quite detached, 49
O son of Kuntī, from the world's affairs,

With self subdued and empty of desire,
Such men as these, renouncing all they have,
Reach that perfection which is free from acts.
Learn, O son of Kuntī, how, in brief, 50
The highest form of knowledge comes to one
Who by devotion is thus purified,
How he attains to *Brahman*, his true Self.
Endowed with reason and in firm command 51
Of his own body and the claims of sense,
With sounds and other objects set aside,
Forsaking love and hate, in solitude, 52
Consuming little, mind and speech controlled,
In constant meditation on the Self,
Dispassionate and free from selfishness, 53
Renouncing pride, assertiveness and lust,
All anger, property and claims of 'mine',
Possessed of only peace, he is prepared
To be the *Brahman*. With his mind at rest, 54
And undisturbed by grief or by desire,
He treats all other creatures as himself
And gives devotion utterly to Me.
By that devotion he becomes aware 55
Of what and who I am; and, knowing this,
He enters into Me. What acts he does 56
He always turns to Me, and by My grace
He reaches that estate which does not change
And never ends. O best of Bhāratas,
Resign to Me the burden of your deeds, 57
And look upon Me as the highest End;
Employing reason, give your heart to Me.

Fix then your mind on Me and, with My grace, 58
You will make light of every obstacle;
But if you will not hear, from stubborn pride,
Why then you will, as certainly, be lost.
If, filled with self-conceit, you dare to say, 59
'I will not fight', your purpose is in vain,
For, come what may, your nature will compel,
And, though delusion prompts you to refuse, 60
You will perform the work ordained by birth,
Fettered, O son of Kuntī, by the law.
Within the hearts of all the Lord God dwells 61
And by illusion makes His creatures move,
As though they ride upon a carousel.
With all your heart resort to Him alone, 62
And by this grace, O Prince, you will obtain
Surpassing peace and your eternal home.
Thus have I offered you these sacred words, 63
A deeper wisdom than the world can know.
Reflect upon it all; act as you wish.
Listen, once more, to what I have to say: 64
With these, My words, the most profound of all,
I bring to you, My dear beloved friend,
The highest good. Devote your thought to Me, 65
Approach Me with your love, bow down to Me,
And offer sacrifice to Me alone,
And you shall reach Me. This I promise you,
For you are dear to Me. Abandoning 66
All actions, good and bad, in Me alone
Seek refuge; do not grieve, and I Myself,
O Bhārata, will free you from all sin.

Never, at any time, may this be taught 67
To any man who lacks austerity,
Or one who does not love, or fails to serve,
Or to a person envious of Me.
Whoever will propound this deepest truth 68
With utter dedication to Myself
To devotees of Mine, shall doubtless come
To Me alone. Who serves Me thus is most 69
Beloved of Me; nor shall there be forever
Born on earth another more beloved.
To study this, our sacred dialogue, 70
I deem to be the worship of Myself;
It constitutes the highest offering,
Prayer of the mind, or wisdom-sacrifice.
Even a man who merely hears these words, 71
If he is full of faith and free from spite,
Reaches, beyond all sin, those glorious worlds
Which harbour those who have lived righteously.
O Pārtha, did you hear what I have said? 72
Has all delusion gone and error fled?"

"Delusion is destroyed", Arjuna cried, 73
"I stand, immortal Lord, freed from all doubt,
For, through your grace, my memory is restored
And, nothing moves me now, except your Word."

Notes on the Text

a

The sound a (a) is the first of the Sanskrit vowels, as it is of the English. It is said to contain the others (i, u, ṛ, ḷ, e, o, ai, au).

Ātman

This may be derived from the root *an*, meaning to breathe. The *Ātman* is the Soul, principle of life, or self of the individual, but at the same time the *Vedic* tradition re-iterates that it is one with the *Brahman*, the supreme God or Self in all creatures (see Notes below).

Aśvattha

The *Kaṭha Upaniṣad* states, "This is the beginningless peepul tree that has its roots above and branches down. That (which is the root) is pure, that is *Brahman* and that is called immortal. On that are fixed all the worlds; none transcends that. This verily is that." (*Kaṭha Upaniṣad,* II.iii.1) On this verse in the *Kaṭha*, Śaṃkara comments: "This tree of the world is an *Aśvattha* - its nature is ever unsteady, like the peepul tree, shaken as it is by the wind of desire and deeds....".

Brahmā

Brahmā is the creator of the universe, one of a triad of divinities, *Brahmā*, *Viṣṇu* and *Śiva* who create, sustain and destroy the universe in their respective roles.

Brahman

Brahman, from the root *bṛh*, means "expansion or growth". It therefore indicates the source of all - a supreme God or Substance, in whom all that exists comes to be, is maintained and is finally dissolved. The *Māṇḍūkya Upaniṣad* states, "All this verily is *Brahman*. This Self (*Ātman*) is *Brahman*", (*Māṇḍūkya Upaniṣad,* II), while the *Taittirīya Upaniṣad* says, "*Brahman* is truth, knowledge and infinite" (*Taittirīya Upaniṣad,* II.i.1). The realisation of an individual's unity with *Brahman* is described as liberation, or *mokṣa*. (See Saṁkara, commentaries on: *Kena Upaniṣad*, Part I, introduction; *Taittirīya Upaniṣad,* II.i.1ff.)

Buddhi

Buddhi, from *budh*, to wake up, observe, is the faculty of mind which determines in observation whether something is true or false, real or unreal. It might be translated as reason, not in the sense of a reasoning process, but rather as that which presents what is true in a given situation. *Buddhi* is also the creative aspect of mind.

Castes

The society of the *Mahābhārata* was based on four distinct castes: *Brāhmaṇas, Kṣatriyas, Vaiśyas* and *Śūdras*. The *Brāhmaṇas*, or *Brāhmins*, were the religious authority, whose duty was to study and teach the *Veda* (see Note below) and conduct religious rituals. The *Kṣatriyas* had political authority and were kings and warriors, while the *Vaiśyas* were traders and conducted business affairs. These three were all called "twice born" because of their initiations into the study of the *Veda*, which were considered second births. The final group, the *Śūdras*, were simply required to serve the other three, and were not permitted to study the *Veda*. (See *Manu* I, 87 ff.)

Dharma

Dharma comes from the root *dhṛ* meaning to support or uphold. It is that which supports society - hence it can mean anything from law and justice to moral duty. A particular aspect of it is *svadharma*, the duty of an individual at a particular time, in a particular place, like Arjuna on the battle-field. It is a central subject in ancient Indian thought, and there are numerous texts which deal extensively with it, not least the *Mahābhārata* itself and the *Manusmṛtti*, or "Laws of Manu."

Dvandva

A *dvandva* is the fifth of the five basic types of compound words identified by the grammarian, Pāniṇi. *Dvandva* compounds are used to form a list. For example, "pleasure and pain" can be written as one word: *sukhaduḥkhe*.

Elements

The creation is said to consist of five elements: Ether (or Space), Air, Fire, Water and Earth. Each of these has its special property: Ether that of sound, Air that of touch, Fire that of form, Water that of taste and Earth that of smell. These are related to the five senses of hearing, touching, seeing, tasting and smelling respectively.

Guṇa

The three *guṇas* are the constituent powers of nature (*prakṛti*). *Sattva* has the quality of clarity and stillness; *rajas* is creative energy, which shows itself as activity and movement; while *tamas* brings activities to a close, in rest and sleep. (XIV)

Holy Way

The path of the realisation of the truth of *Brahman*.

Īśvara

The word *Īśvara* means a lord or prince; hence also the Supreme Being and *Ātman*. (See Note above)

Indra

Indra is the chief of the Hindu deities, and a sky god (cf. Zeus and Jupiter)

Kratu Sacrifice

Kratu is a plan or intention. The *kratu* sacrifice was a sacrificial *Vedic* rite, of which a prime example was the horse sacrifice (*Aśvamedha*), referred to at the very beginning of the *Bṛhadāraṇyaka Upaniṣad* (I,i,1).

Māyā

Māyā, from *mā*, to measure, is the power of illusion, which makes the forms of the Creation appear to have a reality separate from the consciousness which underlies them. Each item is made separate from consciousness by measurement, rather as a pot is made real by the potter's skill as he takes clay, shapes and fires it. The art of the potter has the power of *Māyā*. Hence the whole creation is said to be an illusion playing itself out, like a film on a colourless screen, a screen of unchanging consciousness.

Mantra

A *mantra*, or incantation, was sounded with many sacrifices. There are countless different *mantras*, each with their own specific power. Various systems of meditation also use *mantras*.

Nārada, Vyāsa, Devala, Asita

These were famous sages. Nārada appears in the *Rāmāyaṇa* at the very outset, where he questions the sage, Vālmīki, about the hero, Rāma, and is described as "bull among sages". (See *Rāmāyaṇa*, I, i). Vyāsa is credited with the composition of the *Mahābhārata*.

Nirvana

Literally this means 'blown or put out, extinguished', and whilst it can refer therefore to death or extinction, its philosophical meaning is primarily annihilation of the desires and passions of life and thus perfect calm or repose. The Buddhist scripture, The *Dhammapada*, states that *nirvana* is the highest bliss. (XV, 7)

OM

In the Vedic tradition *OM* is said to be the sound which brings the whole creation into existence, sustains it and dissolves it. The *Māṇḍūkya Upaniṣad* states, "*OM*: this sound is all this. Here is a clear explanation: All that is past, present and future is *OM*. Whatever else there is beyond the three times, that also is *OM*." (*Māṇḍūkya Upaniṣad,* I). It is composed of three sounds *A*, *U* and *M*, which represent the three *guṇas* - *sattva*, *rajas* and *tamas*.

OM, Tat, Sat

Śaṃkara, in his commentary on the *Gītā*, comments on this verse: "*OM, Tat, Sat* traditionally constitute the three-fold name of *Brahman* in the *Vedāntas* (*Upaniṣads*), according to those who know of *Brahman*". For *OM*, see Note above. *Tat* means 'that' or 'essence'; *Sat* means 'existence' or 'truth'.

Progenitors

These were four archetypal men, sprung from the first Man (Manu), who was self-existent. They presided over the earth and its creatures. Their position stemmed from thought directed to the omniscient Lord, whereby they possessed wisdom and power. The present inhabitants of the world are their descendants. (See *Manu* I, 63.)

Puruṣottama

On one level, Arjuna means by this term 'the best of men', since *puruṣa* can mean 'man or person' and *uttama* 'best', but a deeper meaning is the Soul or animating force, and hence *puruṣottama* is the supreme Spirit. The ambiguity precisely represents the fact that Arjuna is addressing Kṛṣṇa both as his charioteer and as an incarnation of God.

Rāma

Rāma is the hero of the great epic, the *Rāmāyaṇa*, in which he destroys the forces of evil in the form of the demon, *Rāvaṇa*, and his followers. He appears in the first book of the *Mahābhārata*, where some of this story is told. He is said to be an incarnation of *Viṣṇu*.

Ṛg Veda

The earliest of the *Vedas*, the *Ṛg Veda*, is a collection of 1028 hymns in praise of the gods. (The root *ṛg* means praise or sacred verse). It is 'the oldest religious text in the world still looked on as sacred' (A.L. Basham).The *advaita* character of it is exemplified in the great '*Hymn of Creation*':

'Then there was neither death nor immortality,

Nor was there then the torch of night and day.

The One breathed windlessly and self-sustaining.

There was that One then, and there was no other.'

(Quoted in A.L. Basham, *The Wonder that was India*, p. 247)

Ṛṣi

By tradition a *ṛṣi* was an inspired sage or seer to whom the *Vedic* hymns were revealed. To say that a *ṛṣi* had said something was equivalent to saying that it was stated in the scriptures. Seven great *ṛṣi* are said to have presided over the first age of creation (*Gītā* X, 6).

Sāma Veda

'The *Veda* of Chants', the *Sāma* is composed almost entirely of *Ṛg Veda* hymns arranged for sacrifices and other rituals. Intoning the *Sāma Veda* in *Vedic* times probably made use of a heptatonic scale and may have been akin to medieval plain chant.

Saṃnyāsin

A *saṃnyāsin* is one who has renounced all worldly possessions, and wanders from place to place with just a staff and begging bowl, relying on alms. This is the final stage of life after that of the student, householder and forest-dweller. A *saṃnyāsin* puts out the fire of his household, which traditionally burned in a house until the head of the household was cremated on it; hence he is not cremated on that fire as others are but is buried.

Soma

Soma juice was the juice from a plant of that name, which was prepared by priests pressing the stalks between stones. This was then sprinkled with water, purified in a strainer and drained into jars. Collected *soma* was mixed with clarified butter and flour, made to ferment, and then offered to the gods in libations.

Śaṃkara

Śaṃkara was the greatest exponent of the philosophy of *Advaita Vedānta*, which states that there is only the one *Brahman* and that all else is but a manifestation of that. He composed commentaries on the *Upaniṣads*, *Gītā*, and *Brahmasūtras*, amongst other works. He is often called the "*Ādiśaṃkārācarya*", because he founded the line of teachers, *Śaṃkārācaryas*, who still exist to this day. Of his dates little is known, although some suggest that he lived in the eighth century AD.

Vasus, Rudras, Aśvins

These are various types of mythical beings. The *Vasus* were a group of eight gods with *Indra* at their head. They were originally personifications of natural phenomena. "*Rudra*" means "crying, howling, roaring, terrific", and it is a name applied to various deities at different times. The *Aśvins* were twin brothers, sons of the Sun who rode in a golden chariot "faster than thought" (*Ṛg Veda*, X, 39, 11). They were benefactors of mankind.

Veda

The four Vedas - *Ṛg, Sāma, Yajur* and *Atharva* - are said to contain all knowledge. The word *Veda* itself comes from the root *vid*, meaning to know. When they were composed is not known; they are said to have been heard by sages, and not to be of human origin, hence they are also called *śruti*, "something heard". They were composed in an early form of Sanskrit, and therefore much of their meaning is not clearly understood. In part they deal with rituals and human action. The *Upaniṣads* are called the *Vedānta*, the goal or end of the *Veda*, as they expound the meaning of the *Veda*. The study and teaching of the *Veda*, as the ultimate spiritual authority, was an essential part of the life of a *Brāhmaṇa*. The *Mahābhārata* was called the fifth *Veda*. (See *Manu* II, 6ff. and other Notes)

Viṣṇu

See Note on *Brahmā*.

Yajur Veda

'*The Sacrificial Veda*' (see Note on *Veda*), is composed of some *Ṛg Veda* hymns, together with prose *Yajus* (sacrificial prayers or formulae), which were pronounced by the priest performing a sacrifice.

Yama

Yama means something which restrains, from the root *yam* (restraining). Hence it is the name of the god of death.

Yogin

Yogin, from the root *yuj* meaning to join, indicates a follower of the Yoga system, or contemplative saint, who is said to be joined with that which he contemplates, which may be *Brahman* itself.

Yuga

The Creation is said to run in cycles of four ages, or *yugas*. By tradition the ages have definite lengths, with a joining period in between each. The process begins with the Golden Age (1,728,000 years), continues with the Silver Age (1,296,000 years) and Bronze Age (864,000 years) and finally ends in the Iron Age (432,000 years). Each represents a fall in the level of consciousness available to Man. (See: *Manu* I, 68-73, 81-86. cf. *Hesiod*, Works and Days, 1.90ff., *Ovid*, Metamorphoses, I, 89ff.)

Notes by David Hodgkinson